Tragedy and Triumph: A North Georgia History Compendium

Christopher Feldt

Published by Christopher Feldt, 2024.

TRAGEDY AND TRIUMPH: A NORTH GEORGIA HISTORY COMPENDIUM

First edition. March 1, 2024.

ISBN: 979-8224908752

Written by Christopher Feldt.

Table of Contents

TRAGEDY

AND

TRIUMPH

A North Georgia History Compendium

Dedication

This book is dedicated to Colonel Sam Tate and the chroniclers of Pickens County history that came before me: Luke Tate, the late Reverend Charles Walker, Robert Scott Davis, Jr. and countless others. Also, to my great professors at college who first and foremost taught me to embrace my curiosity and to question everything I encounter in life. And most importantly, to my daughter Aviana, who gave me a reason to discover who I was, and where I came from.

Foreword

What we know and love as Pickens County was a magical place, literally from its physical beginnings. Located between chains of the oldest mountains in the world, some scenes there have changed little in many thousands of years, even when sabretooth tigers roamed this land. The land is a mineral-rich plateau of aquamarines, graphite, marble, and mica that can be seen for twenty miles before the visitor arrives. Here Georgia's hill country meets the mountains, a land always where different peoples came together with important highways that connect not only places but also the past, present, and future. Since its creation in 1853, Pickens usually was near the bottom of Georgia's 161 counties in physical size and population. Yet, because of its geography many different people arrived; far more cosmopolitan their numbers might imply. With different ambitions, dreams, and realities, their stories sometimes even impacted the nation.

The past of this land and its people, however, became as lost as its gold and silver mines, its prehistoric past, or even the origins of its most colorful names like Long Swamp, Price Creek, and Talking Rock. The late Reverend Charles O. Walker (1929-2010), once a newcomer to the area, began the recovery of that legacy in the 1960s and it is now carried on by people inspired by his work. Chris Feldt now continues this great adventure in ways Charles would have loved. Be prepared on these pages to be amazed as well as entertained! But also, so much more.

Too many places have a history that exists only on paper in archives and books, beyond what can be physically experienced or felt. Chris not only reveals the heritage of this special place, but shows that in Pickens County, William Faulkner's claim, "The past is never dead. It's not even past." is very true! Please take the time to savor the incredible amount of work done here in your own armchair journey to this incredible crossroads of times that have been, are, and will be! Pickens County is always worth any journey!

Robert S. Davis

Author and researcher who has made that trip.

Robert Scott Davis has more than 2,000 publications dealing with genealogy, history, records, and research, most of which deal with the state of Georgia (USA) in some form or fashion. He has been widely quoted by or appeared in CNN, Time, Smithsonian, Newsweek, the Wall Street Journal, and elsewhere.

Introduction

These mountains have their stories. Nearly all of them deal with the relationship between man, his relationship to the earth, and his cohabitation with others. Millions of years ago, when our mountains were under the ocean, the world looked very different. Over time, countless species died, depositing their bones on the ocean floor. Eons of time lapsed, and those calcium remnants had transmogrified into our now famous marble deposits.

Thousands of years before the Europeans found their way to the New World, pre-tribal Indians hunted the backbones of nascent mountains, using the atlatl and other weapons to harvest food. Thousands of years later still, their tribal ancestors shaped the marble into bowls and other tools. They were the first to discover the marble of our region.

Legend tells us that in 1835, an Irish immigrant by the name of Henry Fitzsimmons was traveling by stagecoach along the Federal Road when, after having imbibed a little too much alcohol, was forced to leave a local tavern. It was on this walk that he recognized a shaft of marble rising from the earth. He had been a stonecutter in the Old World, and like one who strikes oil, he embarked upon a journey that would change the path of generations to come.

Henry started a marble industry just east of Jasper in the cove of Long Swamp Creek. There his mining work was begun and the Perseverance Quarry, an apt name for the longevity of the operation, started. Henry's men initially made monuments and gravestones for those in the region. A decade later, Henry was murdered, and ownership of the quarry passed on to others.

In 1850, Tate, Atkinson and Company opened a marble operation at what is now 200 Georgia Marble Road, adjacent to the Tate Mansion. A little over thirty years later, the railroad system found its way to

Tate and Jasper in 1883. The Marietta and North Georgia Railroad extended north from Marietta through Ball Ground, Nelson, Tate and beyond.

A later owner of the Perseverance Quarry, James Harrison of Atlanta, owner of the Atlanta Printing Company, had a successful run at the marble business. Sadly, tragedy struck when James and seven other men were traveling with a marble load from Ball Ground to Tate when a 47-foot-high railroad trestle collapsed killing James and A.C. Gaddis instantly. Several other men, including local Henry Ingram, were seriously injured.

Eventually, the Georgia Marble Company took over. Much has been written in other books about the history of Georgia Marble in the county and of the use of its marble all over the world. But what has been left out was the visionary legacy of Colonel Sam Tate.

From the early 20th Century until his death in 1938 – Colonel Tate forged his empire in Pickens County with reverberations that carried forward well into the future. This book is about that legacy and more: The thread of Colonel Tate's dream as it weaved in and out of sundry lives, enterprises, communities, and America itself.

Other people played important roles in the history of North Georgia. They too have their place in this book.

In the macrocosm, this book contains all the elements of a good story: Heroes, villains, legends and folklore, land barons and shrewd mavericks, success and failure, tragedy and triumph. I leave it to you to decide who or what fits each archetype.

Chris Feldt, Jasper, Georgia, 2024

Fireflies in the Mist

On late summer nights

clouds descend upon the mountains

While storms flashing with lighting

radiate like neon fountains

Within the foggy forests

fireflies luminesce.

forming constellations before us

while attempting to confess

that the forests can be heard talking

of a time that pre-dates man

They were here before you were walking

and your empires were left as sand.

Their choruses are unheard by most,

but the fireflies understand

the cycle of birth, death and ghosts

that haunt our ancient land.

"All is not entropy.", they implore.

"Count their rings if you dare!

Some have 300, and others more

where your forebears once walked there."

The Creeks, DeSoto, the Cherokee,

and their predecessors before

have come and gone like the tides of the sea

to the world of nevermore.

On late summer nights

rain descends from the skies

giving nourishment to the trees

in a forest that never dies.

Part 1

—

THE FIRST INHABITANTS

Ancient Indian Rock Mounds

High atop Rich Mountain there is a half-acre site with 97 stacks of Indian rock piles.

—

Other Sites within Pickens County

Pretribal Indians throughout North America had left remnants of their ceremonial sites in the forms of cairns. According to the Online Etymology Dictionary, a cairn is large, conical heap of stone, especially of the type common in Scotland and Wales and also found elsewhere in Britain, 1530s, from Scottish *carne*, akin to Gaelic *carn* "heap of stones, rocky hill" and Gaulish *karnon* "horn," perhaps from PIE **ker-n-* "highest part of the body, horn," thus "tip, peak" (see horn (n.)). Many of these sites are found in the northeastern part of our nation.

There are examples in Pickens County as well. The most famous being found in Big Canoe at the Indian Rocks Park. Margaret Clayton Russell in 1970 researched the sites found near the location of the Spring that fills Lake Petit. Mrs. Russell determined most of the site to be comprised of archaic Indian artifacts and believed it to be several thousand years old.

According to her research:

Margaret Russell investigated two stone cairns from a cluster of 16 in a section of Pickens County, Georgia, two counties southeast of Murray County. Two other clusters of stone mounds were in the area and there they were located on the east upper slopes of two hills. No artifacts, features or recognizable chemical differences in the soil were found. The landowners had collected a few projectile points in low areas of the property and they fell within the Archaic period from about 7000-2000 B.C. Artifacts made of non-local chert included a small basally notched Eva point, a LeCroy Bifurcated point, a rounded base corner notched early Archaic form and a few flake tools. Items made of quartz, found locally, included a Dalton point, two Big Sandy points; three crude triangular points and several later Archaic points.

A lesser-known site still exists mostly undisturbed today near Sharp Mountain and Rich Mountain. On the side of a hill in a remote location of Pickens County there are 97 stacks of assembled field stones. In 1991, historian Robert Scott Davis, Jr. first wrote about this location in A North Georgia Journal of History Vol. II. These cairns have no apparent arrangement to the order of their placement on the land. Some piles are distributed in a flat arrangement and others are several feet high.

The cairns from both sites look remarkably similar. Both cairn sites are near springs that fed creeks that were affiliated with more modern Indians. One spring was the source of Petit creek which ran near Wolfscratch Village. The other spring – the source of Scarecorn Creek, ran to the village at Murphy Bottoms (Located at the intersection of Scarecorn Creek and Jerusalem Church Road)

A third site containing relics was located within the area now known as Bent Tree. In 1970, anthropologist Robert L. Blakely excavated over seventy sites, finding more than 50 artifacts. All the artifacts found within Bent Tree were from the archaic period and mostly made of quartz. Interestingly there were no examples of pottery found within Bent Tree. Pottery was a much later development within the Indian tribes.

Most people aren't aware of the earliest mention of a location named with present-day Pickens County. History has it that in 1779, General Andrew Pickens (the man for whom our county is named) and several of his soldiers went after the Sharp Mountain village (Cherokee) only to discover that their British agent, Alexander Cameron had escaped. The British had been collaborating with the Cherokee to fight the colonists. This mention of Sharp Mountain is one of the earliest recorded documents regarding Pickens County.

Is it possible that the tribe mentioned in Pickens' writing was the same tribe that resided along Scarecorn Creek? Is there a connection between the location of ceremonial sites being near important sources of water? Most Indians lived in alluvial planes and revered the sun and the water. Why not deem such sources of life sacred? Remarkably, these ancient sites are still beautifully preserved, thousands and thousands of years later, here in Pickens County.

Murphy Bottom – The largest Native American Village Site of Pickens

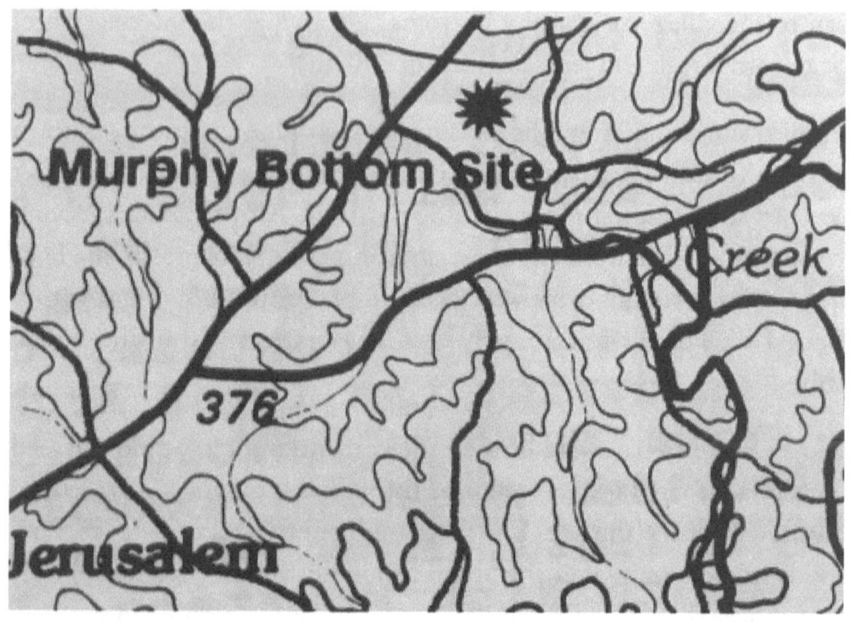

If you ask old-time residents of Pickens County, they'll tell you that Murphy Bottom off Jerusalem Church Road (near two branches of Scarecorn Creek) in West Pickens used to be the place to find arrowheads. Some people mention that a village may have been there at one time.

Archaeology sites in Georgia are labeled in a pattern. This site was originally designated as 9 Pi 12. It also has the designator of 9 Pi 103. It has two designators because it was excavated twice.

In 1956, a man named John Wear, an amateur archeologist from Fairmount excavated the site. He had found the usual suspects: grooved adzes, spades, flint points, checked stamped pottery, and fabric-marked pottery. More interestingly he discovered a refuse pit with burnt corn cobs. Archaic arrowhead points indicate that in the Late Archaic Period this was a great village. A high number of ceramics indicated that site was also occupied much later during the Middle and Late Woodland Periods.

In other words, the Murphy Bottom site was the largest type of excavation of a village site in the county at the time. It helped to differentiate the settlement patterns between the higher mountain elevations and the floodplains. The absence of specific types of pottery and ceramics helped narrow the time range down.

Village life waxed and waned from approximately 3000 BC through around 500 AD. Of course, this would indicate that this was not a Cherokee village nor a Creek village site. This was much earlier.

Interestingly, as discerned from the extensive archaeologic data, the upper reaches of the Scarecorn Creek area (near Rich Mountain) were abandoned or infrequently visited from 1000 AD - 1850 AD.

It should be noted that the original report written by Wear has been lost over time and the only references to it, those by Morse (1960) and Smith, Ledbetter, Wood (1988), etc. are the primary sources of this information.

Long Swamp Town: The History and Origin of Long Swamp Creek

Archaeologist Robert Wauchope's Interpretation of the Mitchell Map

The Mitchell map of 1755 was the first map to show Long Swamp as a place (albeit, under a different name). The map was compiled from the best sources of information at the time under the direction of the Second Earl of Halifax. The map remained one of the largest and most accurate depictions of North America through the 18th Century. At six and a half feet wide and four and a half feet high, it is a massive map.

Portion of the Mitchell Map 1755

The Treaty of Long Swamp

Andrew Pickens

In 1782, an expeditionary force composed of men from Georgia and South Carolina went after a group of Loyalists who were encamped near the Indian town of Long Swamp. Lieutenant Colonel Thomas Waters, the leader of the loyalist group of renegade whites and Indians, fled to Florida. At least 40 of the Indians were killed in the skirmish. Pickens sent three emissaries to get the enemy to surrender in exchange for their prisoners back. After several days, they agreed, and the fighting ended.

Subsequently, the Treaty of Long Swamp was signed on October 17, 1782, between a dozen chiefs, 200 warriors, and Colonel Andrew Pickens, Pickens County's namesake at the helm. This treaty defined the new Cherokee Territory as west of the Upper Chattahoochee River and north of the Savannah River. This battle proved to be the end of all Cherokee incursions into South Carolina and of the Tory attacks. After the battle near Long Swamp, the Cherokee refused to offer the Tories safe harbor.

Willett's Travels

Colonel Marinus Willett

Colonel Marinus Willett was born in 1740 on Long Island. He fought during the Revolutionary War in the Battle of Monmouth in 1788.

In 1790, George Washington sent him as an envoy to the Creek and Cherokee lands (what is now known as North Georgia) to try to keep the peace. The citizens of Georgia were already clamoring for the removal of the native Americans. His journey was successful and 27

Creek Indian leaders came to New York City to negotiate the Treaty of New York, establishing clear boundaries between the Creeks and the Americans.

Colonel Willett left New York on March 15, 1790, headed for Colonel Andrew Pickens plantation in Charleston, South Carolina. He arrived on April 13th and teamed up with a Cherokee named Young Corn to assist with translation.

In his journals, Willet passed through the village of Long Swamp (Neueconoheta) on April 23rd. In Willett's journal, he refers to the town of Long Swamp being on the bank of Hitower, (Hightower/Etowah) and it emptied into the Cousa River. From there he made his way to Pine Log.

Hawkins' Travels

Benjamin Hawkins

Benjamin Hawkins, born in 1752, in North Carolina, came from a wealthy and well-known family. He attended Princeton University and was a Senior classman when the American Revolution began.

George Washington hired him as a French translator. (Hawkins was proficient in French from his studies at school.) Like Colonel Willett, he participated in the Battle of Monmouth during the Revolutionary War.

1796 President George Washington appointed him the Principal Temporary Agent of Indian Affairs South of the Ohio River. In the broadest scope, Hawkins was a peacemaker and was working toward resolving land boundaries between the parties.

According to the *Letters of Benjamin Hawkins, 1796-1806*, Hawkins made his way to Long Swamp (Looccunna Heat) on Tuesday, the 28th of November 1796. He wrote of the remains of an Indian Settlement where only peach trees, cotton stalks, and corn were left behind.

Abandonment?

Whatever caused the village at Long Swamp to be abandoned in the six years between the travels of Willett and Hawkins can only be speculated.

Excavation

Robert Wauchope at Long Swamp Excavation 1939

Fast Forward to 1939, WPA Archaeologist Robert Wauchope excavated Long Swamp Village (CK-1) CK indicates Cherokee County, and the number indicates the first site excavated in the county.

The archaeological evidence showed remnants of a mound at the site, only about 4 feet high. Several houses were found, along with refuse pits, pottery, weapons, tools, animal figurines, arrowheads, and an amulet. The site was occupied on and off from the Early Mississippi Period, until European contact. In short, the archaeological record matches the historical record.

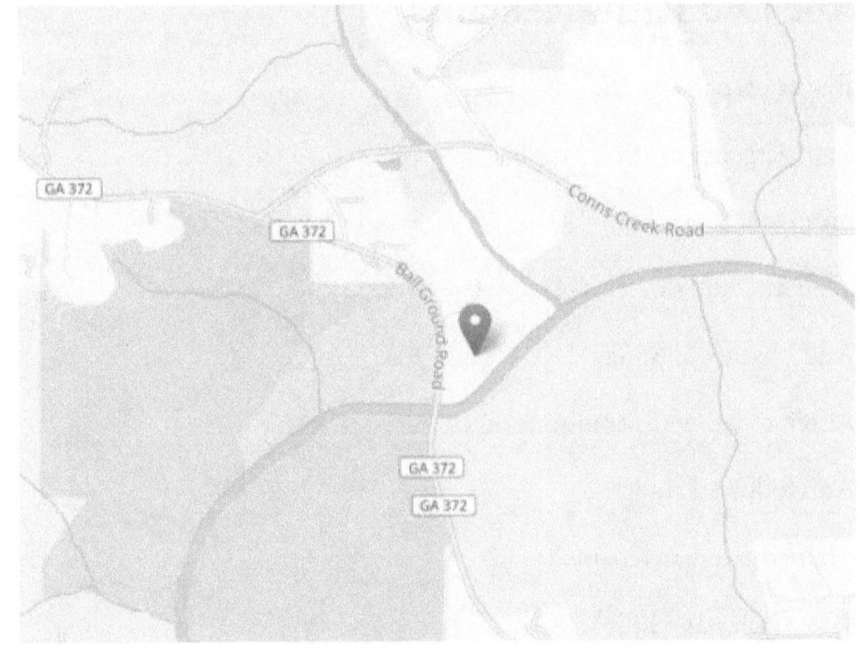

Long Swamp Village's location today

Why Long Swamp?

Dr. John Goff, in his linguistic study, looked at the names Looccunna Heat and Neueconoheta as being Anglicized pronunciations. Sound them out. LO-CUN-NA-HEAT and NOY-CON-OH-HETA. They are quite similar in sound. Dr. Goff went on to explain that gunahita in Cherokee means long. Saluyi is Thicket and part of the word swamp. Goff presumed Long Swamp meant Long Thicket due to the absence of swampland in the immediate area.

NOTE: The Battle of Monmouth was the first successful battle of the Continental Army after the winter at Valley Forge. The British, having taken heavy losses, were forced to retreat. It was this battle that first earned Washington the title of the Father of our country.

The Old Paths Remain

Beside branch and leaf,

a convergence of streams

meanders beneath,

Their ancestor's dreams.

And I bathed in song

Listen to her whispered tone

And followed along

where the Indians roamed:

These valley and hills

in search of big game,

A conquest of kills

for a tribe with no name.

Quartz and rock,

chisel and point,

Hunting the flock

for blood to anoint,

the meal of the past

for a family well fed

in the mountains so vast,

before the Cherokee fled.

Part 2

Enter the Europeans

The Old Federal Road

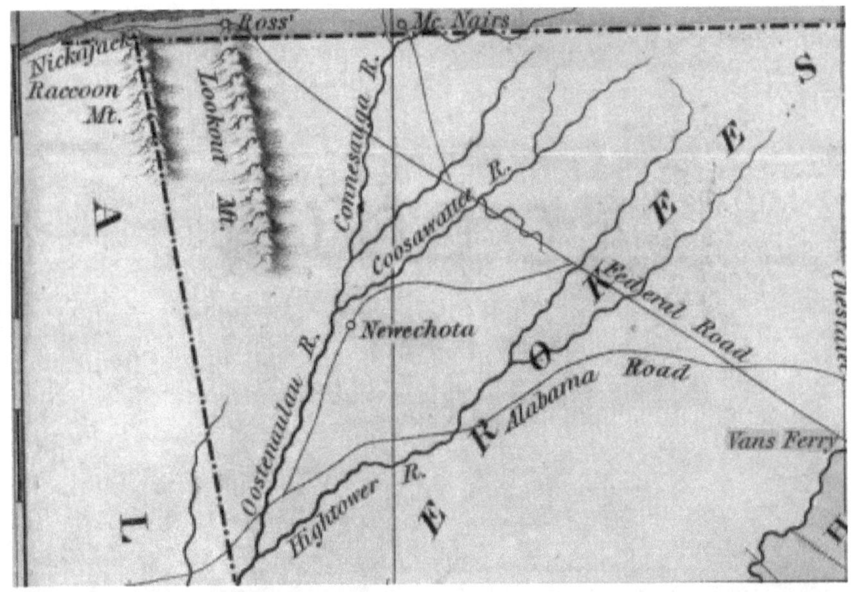

1829 Map showing the Federal Road in Cherokee Territory

The Treaty of Tellico and the great road that traversed Augusta, Georgia to Knoxville, Tennessee.

In 1805 the Federal Road was created, having been established by a treaty between the Cherokee and the United States Government. Chief James Vann, a half Scot, half Cherokee leader.

The treaty allowed for the passage of the white settlers through the Cherokee Territory. A series of taverns and public houses were constructed along different segments providing travelers with a place to rest, and get food and drink. The treaty also allowed for the Cherokee to be the sole operators of such stops.

In the northern part of the Cherokee Territory, Chief James Vann, Chief Daniels, Ambrose and Nancy Harnage (sister of Alexander Sanders), and David and Delilah McNair, operated a series of ferries, taverns, and stands along the road. Starting in Hall County, at the crossing of the Chattahoochee River, Vann had a tavern and operated a ferry for passage.

Vann's Tavern at New Echota

Further ahead, in Forsyth County, Blackburn's Tavern was a way stop. It was at this location where Chief James Vann was shot and murdered on February 20, 1809, in front of his son Joe. It is thought that Alexander Sanders was the man who murdered Vann in retaliation for the abuses he suffered at Vann's hand.

Blackburn's Tavern

Today, the body of Vann lies across the road in Blackburn's Cemetery. It was exhumed twice and not confirmed as being his body. However, he could be buried elsewhere in the cemetery. President James Monroe stayed the evening at the tavern along with John C. Calhoun.

Vann's grave in Blackburn Cemetery

Further up the road, on the southeast side of Long Swamp Creek was the tavern of Chief James Daniels. Chief Daniels had hundreds of acres of land and a two-story house for visitors to stay at.

Artist's rendering of Daniels' Tavern

The last remaining chimney of the Daniels Tavern was photographed in the 1980s

On the southwestern side of the Old Federal Rd, was Harnages. Harnages was run by Ambrose Harnage, a white settler who married Nancy Sanders, the sister of Alexander Sanders. It also served as the first Superior Courthouse of the new Cherokee County in 1832.

Harnage's location, also known as Harnageville, is where the present-day Tate Mansion is in Tate, Georgia.

Artist's rendering of Harnage's Tavern

Next along the road was Taloney/Carmel Mission at Sanderstown. Sanderstown was named for the Sanders family who were the first settlers in what is now Pickens County. The Mission was established in 1819 and stayed active until 1839. It had the first post office, church, and school in (then) Gilmer County. Alexander Sanders was a student there. In 1825 he burned a town hall near there in an act of rage.

The last remaining building of Carmel Mission/Taloney circa 1930

Taloney was a Presbyterian Mission site established in the Cherokee Territory in 1819. It taught the Cherokee and African Americans school and farming basics as well as about the Christian faith. It closed within a year of the Indian Removal in 1839 after Fort Newnan was constructed less than a mile away.

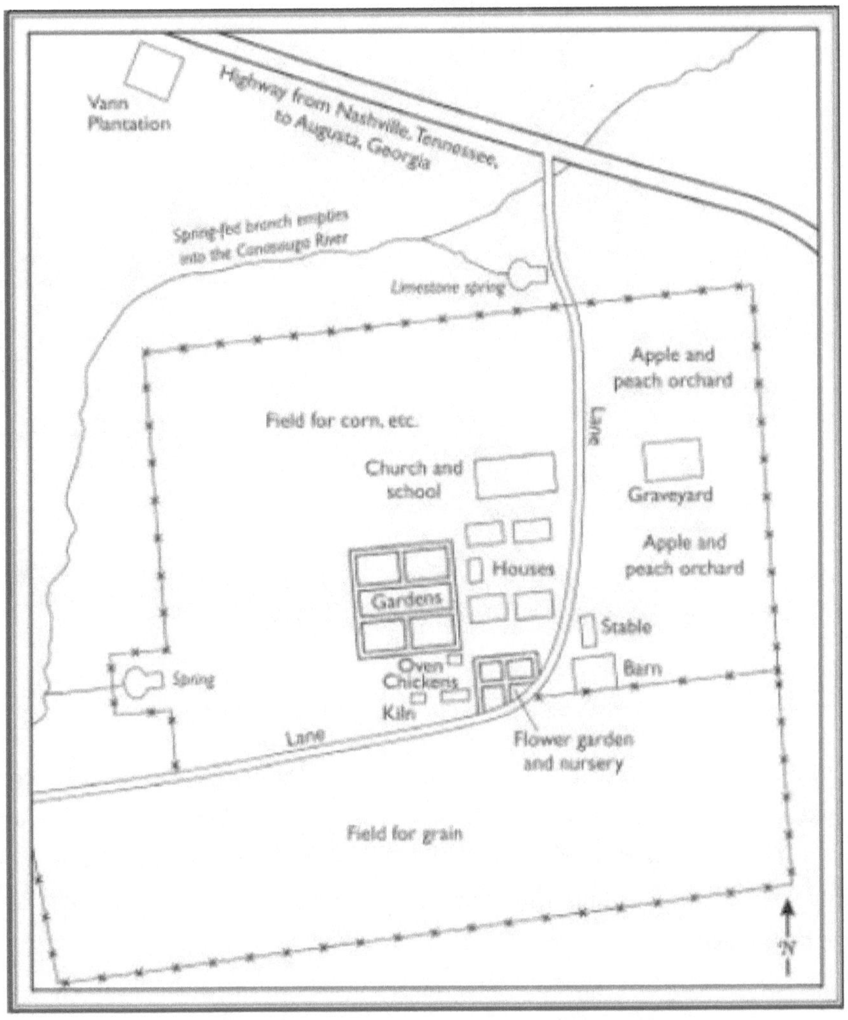

Drawing of the building layout at Spring Place

Spring Place, a Moravian Mission, was established near the location of present-day Chatsworth in 1800. Located within two miles of Chief Vann's brick mansion, it was the first Mission to be established in the Cherokee Territory. Chief James Vann arranged for its placement near his father's town known as Vann's Town, or Vann's Place.

Artist's conception of Spring Place Mission

Finally, as one crossed the border into Tennessee, they reached McNair's Stand, located near the Conasauga River, David McNair, the son-in-law of Chief Vann and Delilah McNair (Vann) operated a house for travelers. It was here the Moravians retreated to after the closure of Spring Place.

Home of David McNair near Tennga, Tenn.

McNair Cemetery - burial place of David and Delilah McNair (Vann)

Vann's daughter, Delilah McNair died on the Trail of Tears. She and her husband David are buried at the site.

The McNair Cemetery today

Sadly, the only remnants of the cemetery are covered by plants on a local farm. The historical marker near the site is missing also. The Tennessee Historical Commission has been notified.

Carmel Station/Taloney: Missionaries among us

Carmel Mission, which took its name on January 7, 1824 - previously named Taloney Mission, was a missionary outpost of the Presbyterians established in 1819 in Gilmer County (present-day Pickens County). The property today is located about two miles northwest of Talking Rock, 12 miles south of Ellijay, just north of 136, and south of Talking Rock Creek by a fifth of a mile on private property. (LL83) Carmel was located near Sanderstown (named after John and George Sanders - wealthy Cherokee landowners)

The last surviving structure of Carmel Mission was seen in 1930

The main building stood until 1919. This was the location of the first school - was started in May 1820, by Moody Hall, the first church (Presbyterian) was built a little later, and post office in Gilmer County.

The Cherokee and African American people attended church services here.

Reverend Samuel A. Worchester, of the Supreme Court case, Worchester vs. United States fame, was a missionary here in January of 1827.

In 1831, Reverand Isaac Proctor was arrested for not complying with the laws regarding white men in the newly annexed part of Georgia. Worchester, Rev. Butler, and others were rounded up and taken to Camp Gilmer located near Hightower.

Among the buildings were a school, a stable, a milk house, a corn crib, a lodging house, a smokehouse, two small houses for pupils, and a 36-foot-deep well.

Carmel Station as seen on the Cherokee County Map from 1832

In 1838, the Indian Removal Fort Newnan/Fort Talking Rock was built on LL 61, located on John Sanders's property. Today the site of the Indian Fort is located immediately east of the Blaine Masonic Lodge on the corner of Antioch Church Road.

The mission was closed in 1839 because of the tumultuous Indian Removal.

The Resurrection of the Nelson-Simmons Tavern

In 1804, the Cherokee Indians had negotiated the terms of the creation of a Federal Road that ran between Tennessee to Augusta, Georgia.

TRAGEDY AND TRIUMPH: A NORTH GEORGIA HISTORY COMPENDIUM

In exchange for settlers' passage through the Cherokee Territory, the Indians were allowed to operate taverns along their old Cherokee highway.

In less than 30 years, in 1832, the Cherokee Territory was mapped out at the request of the government with the purpose of dividing the land into lots, giving away lots by a lottery system creating counties of governance under the control of the state of Georgia.

There were three taverns located in the land that now comprises Pickens County. The Daniel's Tavern - (formerly located east of Long Swamp Creek on the north side of Hwy 53) and Harnage's, located where the Tate Mansion presently is. The third tavern was the Nelson-Simmons Tavern located just northwest of Jasper, just east of the Volkswagen repair shop on Talking Rock Road.

By 1832, the infamous Colonel Haney Nelson was operating a tavern about four miles southeast of the Carmel Mission site. He also was listed as a Postmaster of Talking Rock for about a year and a half (although he wasn't living in Talking Rock)

NOTE: In 1830, Colonel Nelson was involved with the fort near the Frogtown/Hightower area. (Matt Hwy - Forsyth County) The State of Georgia had established Camp Eaton/later Camp Gilmer to protect the newly discovered gold mines in Cherokee County.

Nelson was Postmaster from 18 January 1832 -15 July 1833

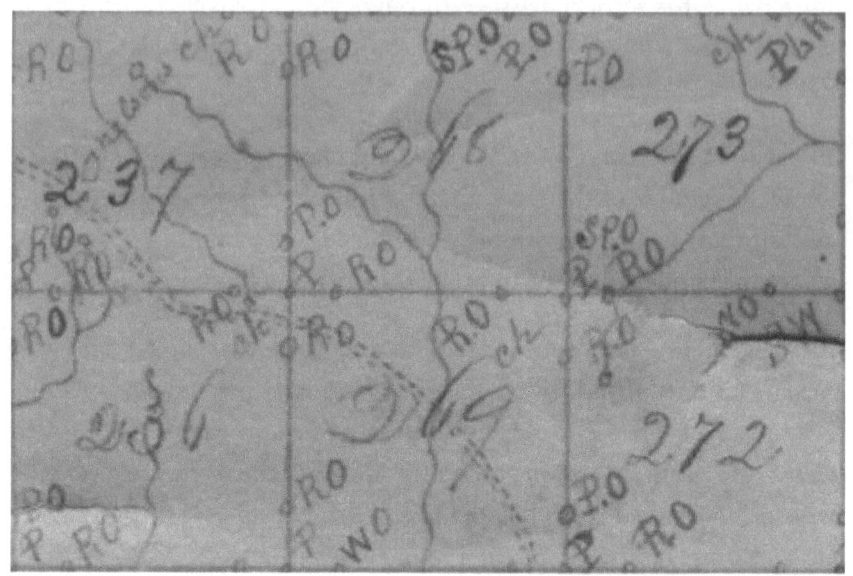

Nelson's as seen on the 1832 map of Cherokee County (LL 237)

In 1835-1836, Nelson was one of the last Indian Agents (a non-native agent tasked with assimilation) who was keeping Georgia Governor Lumpkin appraised of the lands that had been evacuated by the Cherokee. (He also was involved with the harassment and arrest of missionaries at New Echota and he had previously tried arresting Reverend Isaac Proctor at Carmel Mission in 1831.) Colonel Nelson also was the second in command under General Winfred Scott for the Indian Removal that took place in 1838. Col. Nelson sold his tavern to James Simmons, an Indian trader, who was shown on the 1840 census of Gilmer County. Nelson later relocated to Gordon County.

Unlike the former tavern owner, James Simmons was a kind man and operated a thriving trading post out of the Tavern. A microfiche of his trading ledger is located at the Pickens County Library. Eventually, he even used the tavern location as the post office named Marble Head.

Marble Head as seen on Mitchell's 1860 map of Georgia

He did this for four years, between 1850 and 1854. (It should be noted that many Post Offices in Georgia in the 19th Century were located in Dogtrot-style homes as the Tavern because having an open breezeway left a dry place to leave postage.

James Simmons was postmaster from 5 July of 1850 - 3 June 1854

Simmons frequently interacted positively with the Cherokee before they had been forced to leave. A story recounting an Indian Ball Game (Anetsa) he witnessed on the neighboring property of Hood's Field, was published in Belle K. Abbott's book *The Cherokee Indians in Georgia.*

Later, during the Civil War, James became a member of Georgia's Secession Delegation and was one of eight members who voted against Georgia leaving the Union. He was quoted as saying *"I thought secession would involve us in war and was too hasty."*

In his old age, James sold the land for the Jasper City Cemetery in 1887 and 1891. He passed away at the age of 91 in 1894.

In 1903, the tavern location is shown as Simmons Place (LL 237) on the J.W. Henley map of Pickens County.

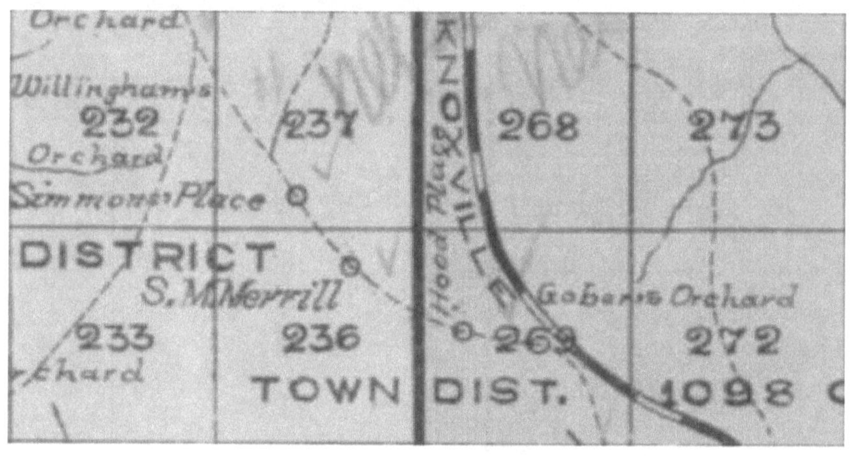

Simmons Place as shown on the 1903 map (LL 237)

Eventually, the land passed into the hands of the Trippe family (heirs of the Simmons family) around 1898 before moving to the Stanfield family (also Trippe relatives) sometime after Miss Susie Trippe died in 1977.

In 1997, the Marble Valley Historical Society attempted to salvage the site. Sadly, although they had the impetus, they were never able to salvage the property which by that time had been recently hit by a tornado and fallen into disrepair.

In 2004, the final owner of the tavern property, who had grown tired of paying taxes, agreed to privately sell the wood and fieldstone from the tavern to a private owner named Clyde Smith. Clyde had previously restored and built other historic cabins across North Georgia. He placed a small ad in the Atlanta Journal and Constitution for a cabin for sale. And fortunately for all of us, Phyllis Clark, a woman from Atlanta who loved history, decided to do what the Historical Society could not. She would save the Nelson-Simmons Tavern, even if it had to be moved and rebuilt.

In fact, according to famed historian Robert Scott Davis, Jr., "The original Pickens County Historical Society, with J.B. Hill (1903-1991, former monument designer and friend of Colonel Sam Tate and Luke Tate) among its members, specifically was formed to save the Simmons House....This group preceded the creation of the Marble Valley Historical Society (1980) by a few years."

With the purchase from Mrs. Clark, for around $20,000, she had Clyde rebuild it at an undisclosed location in a remote wilderness section of Pickens County. Clyde had labeled all of the pieces from the cabin that were salvageable and diagrammed a plan.

CHRISTOPHER FELDT

The Tavern was reconstructed in 2004

The current front of the rebuilt tavern with a door that converts the former dogtrot breezeway into an enclosed foyer

The tavern in the 1970s with the open breezeway

Imagine my excitement learning of the tavern's continued existence! Upon reaching out to the owner, they expressed willingness to have me share in their history by teaching the readers of the Pickens Progress that a lost part of our legacy wasn't lost after all.

I recently had the honor and privilege of meeting the owners. Out of respect for the current occupants, I'll only share a few of the photos I took while at the site. However, I will include many photos from the building project that were provided to me.

The original tavern as seen from the rear, looking through the dogtrot breezeway

A close-up of the salvaged door from a Civil War period piece from Social Circle, GA

The inside of the foyer area (first-floor interior of the tavern)

The first-floor living room

The first-floor dining room

CHRISTOPHER FELDT

The upstairs bedroom

The loft section above the main room

This is a departure from the original closed-floor design

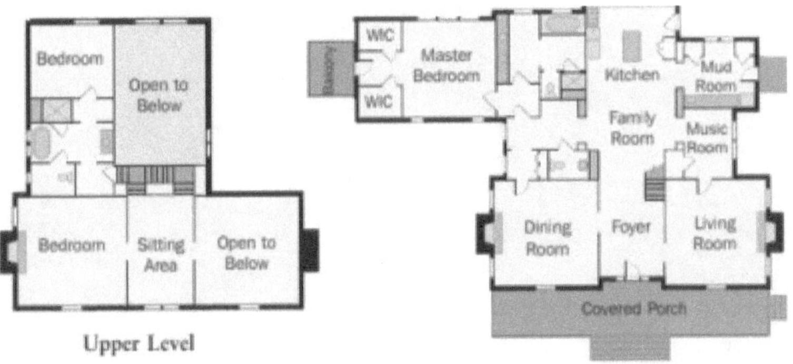

The yellow portion of the plan represents the section of the dogtrot that was salvaged.

The portions behind are of the expansion to make the property more spacious.

After Clyde Smith rebuilt the first and second floors of the tavern, an architect was called to build an expansion. Most of the expansion would be located off the back of the original tavern. The entire house is a work of art and won a prestigious AIA (American Institute of Architects) award.

It should be a point of interest, that the first forefather of the Clark family who arrived here was an Irish Stonemason who directly worked for Governor Wilson Lumpkin in the construction of his brick mansion that currently resides on UGA property. The irony is that the first occupant of the tavern, Charles Haney Nelson, also routinely reported to Governor Lumpkin.

Mrs. Clark's dream came true. Sadly, not long after the property was completed, she tragically passed away. Today, the property remains in her family, as a lasting reminder of her vision, history, and of the beauty of the human spirit.

The Forgotten Game of Anetsa

The Game of Anetsa - The Little Brother of War

Anetsa, a game that resembles lacrosse, was a Cherokee Indian game played by two teams of up to eighteen players on a 100-yard field. Normally this was played by a water source. They used wooden sticks (longer than a tennis racquet) with a depressed cavity made of deer sinew (looking similar to a spoon) On each end of the field, there were two poles erected with a pole spanning the top (similar to Football posts). The first team to twelve points (points were earned by running a ball through the poles) would win. There was no time limit on the games. The ball was not allowed to be touched by the hands of the players. There were no penalties for holding, but the players would cover themselves in a slippery substance from a plant, or with bear grease to ensure that 'holding' wouldn't be easy. The game was known as the little brother of war because in many ways it was an aggressive game. It was also used to solve disputes. If a dispute arose among different groups of natives, they would frequently play to resolve the issue.

Anetsa field and equipment drawing by Charles O. Walker

According to the late Reverend Charles O. Walker, there were other locations where this game was played locally. One of the ball fields is located on the former grounds of the Griffeth family on the present land of the Episcopal Church of the Holy Family. The most famous local site is of course in Ball Ground, Georgia, where a game was used to settle a territorial dispute between the Cherokee and the Creek Indians. **NOTE:** As a point of interest, Ball Ground appears as Battle

Ground from maps dating back to the 1800's. Some people think this name refers to the alleged battle of Taliwa (1755).

According to Belle K. Abbot, in her book 'The Cherokee Indians in Georgia', one day in the early nineteenth century, James Simmons (owner of the former Tavern located on the Federal Road - located near the present Vintage Volkswagen shop across from NZI Services) witnessed teams from the Indian Districts of Coosawattee and Hickory Log competing in Hood's field (A.K.A. Hood's Place - see LL 269, District 12, of J.W. Henley's map of Pickens County from 1903). Hood's Field was very close to his Tavern on the Old Federal Road.

By 1867, the Hoods owned over 300 acres of land in District 1098. Jesse Hood was listed as living in Gilmer County, at the site of what is now Pickens County as early as 1840. (Two years after the Indian Removal took place.

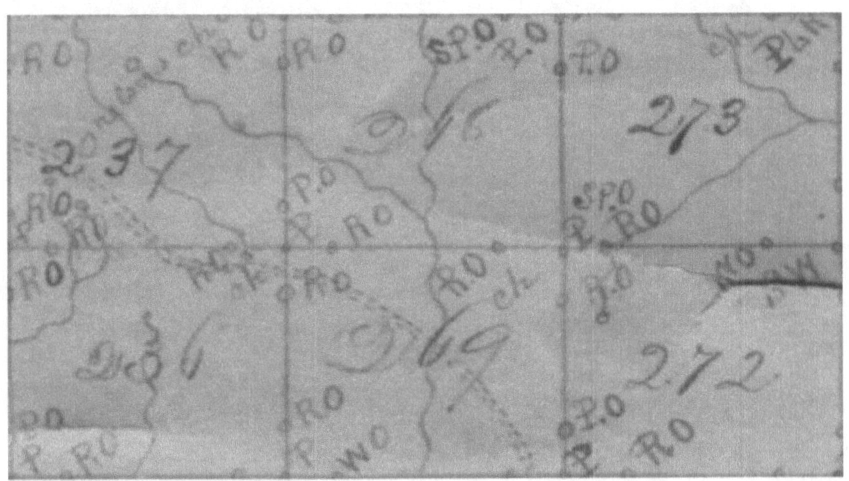

1832 Cherokee County Map

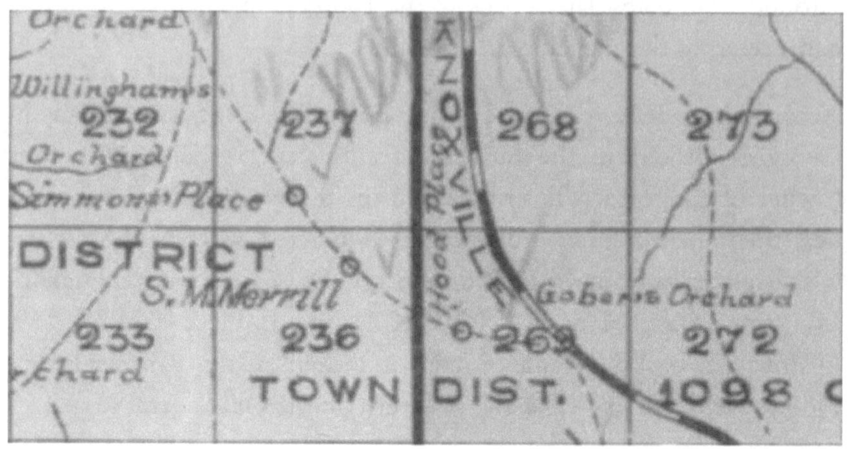

1903 Pickens County Map (NOTE: Simmons Place is same location as Nelsons)

Hood's Field/Place near Town Creek or branch streams

The game between the two tribes took two hours to complete, and in the end, the team from Coosawattee won the day.

Regardless of the exact locations of the ball fields, we definitively know the game was played throughout the Cherokee Territory and on the land that now makes up Pickens County. As for the idea of having a game settle disputes between political parties, I'm all for it.

Fort Newnan/Fort Talking Rock: Indian Removal Fort

Fort Newnan was built in March of 1838 in Gilmer County (Present-day Pickens) It was named after Major General Daniel Newnan, Georgia Secretary of State of the 1820s.

The Fort was led by Captain Reverend John Dorsey. He led a mounted regiment. On May 26, 1938, After the Indian removal was completed, Captain Dorsey refused to give up the post. A detachment was sent to arrest him, but by their arrival, he had gone home, and half of his men had left. The remainder of his troops were labeled as a complete mob. Dorsey's unit was mustered out by June of 1838.

Drawing of Fort Newnan by Reverend Charles O. Walker

The fort was built in Land Lot 61, District 12, of Cherokee County. The fort was located off the Federal Road near John Sanders's home in Sanderstown, and not far from Taloney Mission.

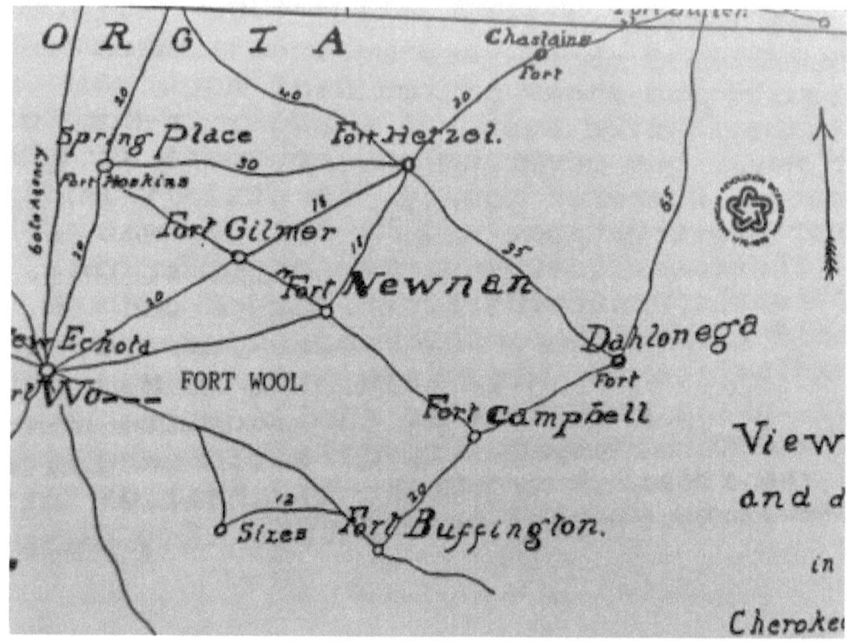

Today, the location of Fort Newnan is located just east of the Masonic Lodge in Blaine, Pickens County, Georgia. It is located near the corner of Antioch Church Road and Highway 136. The graves of the Cherokee are located behind a fenced area on privately owned land

Fort Newnan Grave Site 2023

The Menagerie

Within each of us are dark places,

caverns of pain and loss

of fear and insecurity,

where we cautiously explore

the depths of our burrows;

making mysteries intelligible

and our secrets known,

by bringing each artifact

into the light of day

and illuminating a complete

diorama of ourselves.

Thereby filling our galleries

with reclaimed thoughts:

our museum of antiquities

our menagerie of memory.

Part 3

Moonshining and Outlaws

The Night Riders of Pickens County (Part 1)

During the Civil War and for several decades that followed, criminals and vigilantes from various places around the United States would don Klan-like outfits and terrorize citizens. In many newspapers, they were commonly referred to as Night Riders. They were named after their preferred time to commit crimes while on horseback.

The Night Riders, like the Home Guards, gangs, and Irregular units of the Confederate Army, frequently harried and preyed upon law-abiding citizens in the power vacuum created by the War and the collapse of the South.

Civil War Operations in Pickens County

In 1864, the Union Army sent men into what is now the Talking Rock area of Pickens County to apprehend wanted men. They apprehended A.J. Green and damaged his property. Later, when the Army went after James Simmons, they were scared off by the Jordan Gang.

The Night Riders of Pickens County

Honest Man's Friend and Protector outfit

More than a decade later, during the Moonshine Wars of the 1870s, frequent clashes between revenuers, moonshiners, informants, and the U.S. Army happened throughout Pickens, Gilmer, and Fannin Counties. An investigation was launched and the results essentially laid blame on the unscrupulous tactics of the Deputy Marshals who overzealously went after whomever they felt.

In 1886, Pickens County resident, David C. Wheeler, formed a vigilante group (the group's name has been lost to time) that committed arson against informants. In 1886 they burned down the house of A.J. Holder and in 1887 the house of N.C. McClain.

The Honest Man's Friend and Protector

Later, in 1889, twenty-six men gathered together (including D.C. Wheeler) to carry their tradition of vigilantism. This time they called themselves The Honest Man's Friend and Protector (hereafter referred to as the HMFP), and drew up a manifesto that outlined their mission. Each of them planned to assume the name of an honorable resident of Pickens County who was known to be against moonshining. And if they were caught, they hoped to damage the reputations of their nemesis, or at the very least, cause one to question the reputation of those upright citizens.

The home of John R. Aiken was burned to the ground on November 12th, 1889. He, his wife, and his children were left homeless as a result. John was formerly a witness against one of the HMFPs in a revenue case.

On December 3rd, 1889, the HMFP gathered in a valley just east of Sharptop Mountain at the Thomas W. Fields property. Tom, his cousin Eli Fields, and the other men, donned their black robes and hoods and launched a brief reign of terror. They burned down the homes of other citizens who had turned evidence against them. One of the arsons happened on Jones Mountain at the residence of Mr. Nelson Ledford. Mrs. Ledford was home with her children when they were accosted. In short order, the Ledford barn and house were razed to the ground.*.

A third arson happened in mid-December, 1889, when the HMFP burned down the house of Mike Stoner.

Shortly thereafter, Sheriff Johnson and Deputy Marshalls Lee Cape (one of the falsely listed members on the manifesto) and Mann tracked down two of the men, James Coffey and W.T. Champion. The two men were released after a preliminary trial.

After the men were caught, one of the members named Coffey spoke of the group's intent and told the authorities where to find their manifesto. It was found in a hollowed-out oak tree in a cigar box that was wrapped with one of the black hoods of the Night Riders.

It was scrawled on a piece of foolscap paper* and read:

(**NOTE:** I left all the original misspellings to convey the actual handwritten message)

"Honest Man's Friend and Protector

We, Nelson Ledford, John Hayes, Mike Stoner, William Bradley, Isaac Southern, G.N. McPherson, John R. Aiken, John Brock, Bob Black, James Dobson, Thomas Hayes, John McPherson, Will Thomas, Samuel Parker, Thomas Hamilton, George Leak, Joseph Mullinax, Joe Padget, Samuel McClain, Lee Cape, Marion Blackwell, Griff Cason, Thad Padget, Bill Bradford, Jim Chadwick, Cornell Pace and Wheeler Burlison do solemnly swear that we will protect each other in putting down reporting, and that we will stick to each other in anything we under take, and we will be true to each other at all times and in all troubles, we or any of us may get in to in regard to this matter, and that we will allways be reddy to help our kind when we are cald upon, and in case any of us should be deprived from this privilege we will do all that we can all that we can to get him out of his or there trubble, and further say that we will not take in any person or persons without concent of all the party, and that we will do all we can to keep down suspition, and that we will be detectives for each other at any and all times and will work for the good of our country, and expresly for ourselves; and we further swear that if any many devulges any of the secrets of the honest man's friend and protector, the final event of his conviction shal be sentence of death in any way the true party thinks best; and we further swear that we will all ways be ready to work when cald upon when in power to do so, and futher swear that we will always do justice between all parties and will be kind to each other and help each other in bearing the burdings of life, and if any of the party gets so far away that he can not be with the party or is ever excluded fom this band that he will keep the secrets of this body as secret as a member in full command. We do solemnly swear that we will do all the things in the above stated case as we can at any and all times. SO HELP US GOD!"

After the arsons happened the authorities began looking for the rest of the group. Jack Lansdown, John Forrester, and Jim Wiggington were arrested by R. Henderson and William Dooley.

Wigginton was released for promising to turn on his fellow conspirators.

- Most citizens in the area were happy the HMFP was brought to justice. Although there were more than a few people who felt they were innocent. Some of those opposed broke into the Pickens jail and set Lansdown and Forrester (along with two other non-members of the group, free)

Lansdown was apprehended shortly after that.

The names of the HMFP are:

Jack Lansdown, Sr. - Captain

D.C. Wheeler - First Lieutenant

George Fields - Second Lieutenant

Jack Lansdown, Jr.

Seaborn Lansdown

Eli Fields

Thomas Fields

Johnny Fields

William Fields

Tom M. Pendley

Carter Pendley

Cicero Padgett

Harrison Jones

Arch Grizzle

Jim Wiggington

Jack Forrester

John Coffey

George Coffey

Patton Millice

Tom Rollin

M.G. Holbert

Joe Richards

Alexander Richards

The sensational nature of the story made it into newspapers all over the country. Soon trials were initiated and seven of the HMFP were given life prison sentences by Judge Gober.

Judge George Franklin Gober

Aftermath

Eli Fields - A few years later after being incarcerated, was pardoned. He and his wife Rachel relocated to a 100-acre parcel near Hendrix Mountain, and they raised nine children. Eli, like his father before him, was one of the best distillers around. He and his children made moonshine and apple brandy from their apple orchard.

Eli Fields' home was located near here. 9th hole of Bent Tree's Golf Course

In June of 1891, two of the men, Seaborne and Jack Lansdown, attempted to break out of their imprisonment. Jack was killed in the escape attempt from the Dade Coal facility. Seaborn managed to escape, but having been shot in the thigh, was recaptured. He likely absconded to his remote property in Northeast Pickens in the area known as the Lansdown.

Lansdown Chimney north of Wheeler Cabin Road

Later he escaped again, assumed a new name, and moved out of Georgia.

Thomas Monroe Pendley was later pardoned and moved into the Griffeth Property off the Jasper-Dawsonville Road (Cove Rd). He moved into the dog trot home that was built in 1877 by Samuel Tate's cousin Caleb. Thomas remodeled the home and lived the rest of his days as a landowner and farmer.

Griffeth- Pendley Dogtrot - One time home of Tom Pendley

The Next Generation

Years later, Eli Fields' son, Walter, carried on Eli's legacy. One day, teenage Walter lost his leg while trying to board a train and began moonshining to make a living. Walter became "Peg" (pronounced "Pag"), named after his conspicuous appendage. He continued making liquor and became one of the last genuine old-time whiskey makers in the North Georgia region. Peg Fields died in 1977.

Walter "Peg" Fields

- In 18th Century England, paper was produced with the watermark of a fool's cap, a jester hat
- See more on Nelson Ledford in Part 2

The Night Riders of Pickens County (Part 2) The Enigmatic Andrew Jackson Glenn

During the heart of the Civil War, Pickens County was torn between sides. The flag that flew over the courthouse yard was a Union flag. Yet, many of the residents fought on each side. Many of the Darnell family fought for the North, while those from the Fields side predominantly fought for the South. And while many neighboring counties were far more aligned with the Confederacy, as with Pickens's history with race and slavery, Pickens was more of a mixed bag.

There were only a few notable incursions by the Union Army into Pickens County. One was near Hinton when soldiers exacted revenge on two of McCollum's Scouts. Several others happened near Talking Rock. In each instance, Home Guards like the Jordan Gang, McCollum's Raiders, or Irregular Units like the Pickens Raid Repellers were involved.

Earlier in August of 1863, A.J. Glenn, having recently enlisted in the Pickens Raid Repellers, had his tanyard raided by a dozen pro-union women, who ran off with "as much leather as they could well carry off." According to Glenn, they intended to steal rather than work for the rest of the war so they could live as well as men like Glenn. The women stated they wished the Yankees would win the war.

Later, in early June of 1864, Andrew Jackson Glenn and two other men were captured by Union forces from the 3rd Kentucky Cavalry near Talking Rock Creek. Other people were shot at, however, none were injured. A.J. Glenn, now a member of the local Confederate Irregular Unit called the Pickens Raid Repellers, also happened to be a major landowner in the county. In this same raid, Union Forces went after James Simmons, but the Jordan Gang thwarted them.

Federal Raid in Pickens County.

Correspondence Augusta Chronicle.

MARBLE WORKS Pickens county, June 6.—The Yankees made a raid, on Thursday, on Talking Rock creek, some miles above Jasper Court House, Ga. They captured three men named Glenn.—Peoples and Stiles; also some negroes, wagons, mules, horses and provisions,

They are said to have been Kentucky cavalry and to number about six hundred men,

Several citizens were shot at, but none of those fired at were either hurt or captured.

We have no forces in this section. The people are very much frightened, and are moving off south and west.   S.

Daily Columbus Enquirer, June 12, 1864

Another Instance happened near Marble Hill when General Joseph Wheeler's men came into the county in mid-August of 1864 and resulted in two deserters being killed in what is known as the 'Covington Hang' on Four Mile Road.Different reports at the time mention as many as 400 Yankees being captured in Pickens County. Other reports mention the Home Guard units of Dawson and Pickens County in a bad light.

In August 1865, Berry and Boswell Collins were murdered in Hinton for their connection with McCollum's Scouts.

A.J. Glenn and his first wife

Glenn was later released and came back to Pickens County. He drops from the historical record until about a decade later. Then in 1877, partially in response to the death of Army Lieutenant Augustine McIntyre in Fannin County, an investigation was launched into the relationship between the military, revenuers, government agents, moonshiners, and citizens.

Col. Sam Williams was placed in charge of the investigation by the Legislature of Georgia. After interviewing 100s of people, his conclusions largely placed the blame on the actions of unscrupulous Deputy Marshalls in their overzealous pursuit of tax enforcement.

The most infamous of which was Deputy Marshall Charles B. Blacker. Beginning in the early 1870s he worked for the State of Georgia. Sometimes marshals assisted revenue agents and other times they acted as revenue agents.

In 1876 Blacker ordered revenue agents and soldiers from Fort McPherson, under the command of Lieutenant McIntyre to a suspected still site at John Emory's house near the Santa Luca area of Gilmer County. Several people were detained at the site when Mr. Emory approached and instantly was shot dead by Private William O'Grady. Blacker's men hid the body and left.

O'Grady was to be tried in Atlanta but was transferred to the Federal Court's Custody at the request of Ulysses S. Grant. Later in the U.S. District Court, O'Grady was found innocent and set free.

In 1877, Deputy Blacker led a small military contingent to the home of a suspected moonshiner in Fannin County. Blacker didn't bring a warrant (as was his normal practice) to the home of Ayers Jones. She and her children were home alone when Blacker and the U.S. Army soldiers came. There was an argument at the house when the moonshiners approached from the outside. Not knowing who was in the house harassing the woman and children, the moonshiners angrily and defensively approached. A gunfight ensued and Lieutenant McIntyre was mortally wounded and left behind.

In 1877, Deputy Marshal Blacker, and A.J. Green were both interviewed by Col. Williams.

Beginning in 1873, several residents of Pickens and Gilmer County reported being visited by Deputies and having their stills destroyed. Subsequently, to help them avoid consequences from Deputy Blacker and others, A.J. Green would suddenly show up on their street and "negotiate their freedom from trouble" for cash. In a case involving Samuel Taylor of Pickens County, Green even demanded the distiller bring whisky and money to Deputy Blacker as payment. Taylor claimed the Commissioner from Cartersville, Aaron Collins, had sold him three stills, which he in turn, sold to Nelson Ledford, Mr. Frix, and another man.

Green had connections. This shady activity was mentioned over and over in Col. Williamson's report. Green himself admitted to collecting cash from people to assist them and admitted to not being a lawyer. In testimony, United States Commissioner, Judge Aaron Collins freely admitted to selling stills to A.J. Green.

One of the men who testified against A.J. Green, and mentioned Green's receipt of illicit moonshine stills, was Nelson Ledford. The very same man whose house was burnt down by the HMFP some 12 years later. Incidentally, Nelson Ledford also was accused of receiving stills from Mr. Turner, who had gotten them from the United States District Commissioner in Cartersville, Judge Aaron Collins.

It should be noted, that of all the people Col. Williams interviewed in Fannin, Gilmer, and Pickens County, he was only treated unpleasantly by one person. A.J. Glenn.

I cannot conclude this already very lengthy report without saying that, notwithstanding I went into the counties of Gilmer, Fannin and Pickens, a perfect stranger, and the people in a great state of excitement, I was alwas received with the utmost kindness, and treated with all the hospitality that one could expect or desire.

From the time I arrived at Ellijay, and made known the object of my visit, every official and citizen there expressed not only a willingness but a desire to help me to put before you a true statement of the condition of affairs in their county—many men giving up business to assist me when I so desired.

In this and Fannin counties I spent most of my time, as most of the recent arrests were made there. But the same I have said of Gilmer I most cheerfully repeat as to Fannin and Pickens, with one exception in Pickens, and that was at the house of A. J. Glenn. This was after I had shown him my authority as given me and explained the reasons of my visit. As I had never seen him before, I can only imagine that the position he occupied, as given in the statements of Mr. Holt and others, was the cause, if any, for his having treated me in any other way than politely.

Atlanta Constitution, May 8th, 1877

Aftermath

As a result of Williams's report and the outrage of Georgia Governor Colquitt, the Posse Comitatus Act was passed, placing restrictions on when the military would be allowed to be used in civilian matters.

A.J. Green

A.J. Green was never tried or arrested for any wrongdoing. He ended up leaving Georgia permanently and settled in Erath County, Texas. He donated land to create the Bluff Dale Tabernacle, to expand the newly renamed Glenn Cemetery in Hood County, (where A.J. and his family are buried), and other land in Bluff Dale, Texas. A.J. Green died in 1901.

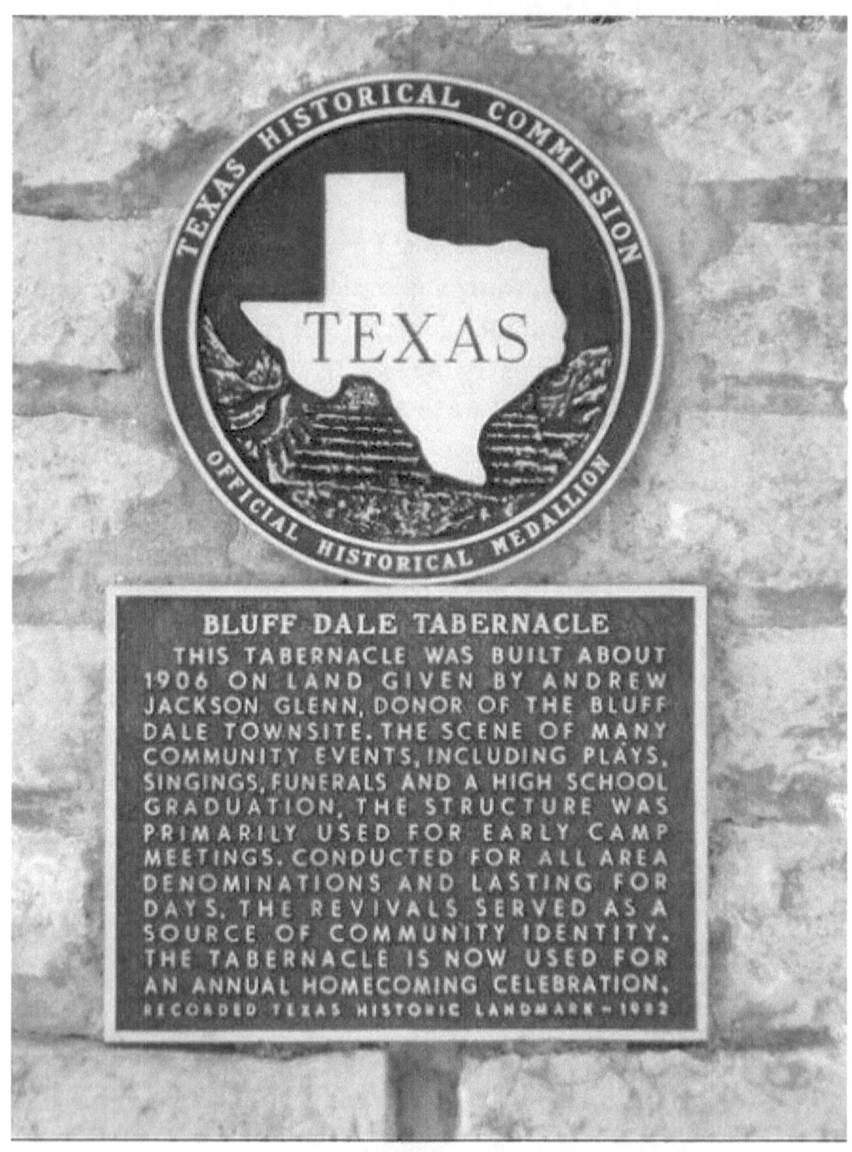

TEXAS HISTORICAL COMMISSION
TEXAS
OFFICIAL HISTORICAL MEDALLION
BLUFF DALE TABERNACLE
THIS TABERNACLE WAS BUILT ABOUT
1906 ON LAND GIVEN BY ANDREW
JACKSON GLENN, DONOR OF THE BLUFF
DALE TOWNSITE. THE SCENE OF MANY
COMMUNITY EVENTS, INCLUDING PLAYS,
SINGINGS, FUNERALS AND A HIGH SCHOOL
GRADUATION, THE STRUCTURE WAS
PRIMARILY USED FOR EARLY CAMP
MEETINGS. CONDUCTED FOR ALL AREA
DENOMINATIONS AND LASTING FOR
DAYS, THE REVIVALS SERVED AS A
SOURCE OF COMMUNITY IDENTITY.
THE TABERNACLE IS NOW USED FOR
AN ANNUAL HOMECOMING CELEBRATION.
RECORDED TEXAS HISTORIC LANDMARK - 1982

Charles Blacker

Charles Blacker was shot in a confrontation with Cumming, GA tavern owner, Harrison Barker.

Shortly after he retired from the Marshals Service, moved to Pennsylvania, where he died in 1919.

Judge Aaron Collins and his wife were nearly murdered in January of 1886, when his home was dynamited by moonshiner Tobe Jackson, from Bartow County.

Aaron was born in North Carolina and immigrated to the Scarecorn Creek/Blaine/Talking Rock area by a wagon train of seven siblings and their children. His father, William James Collins was one of the wealthiest men in 1860 Pickens County. Aaron later sat on the second Petit Jury of Pickens County's first court session. The two men killed at the church in Hinton in 1865, Berry and Boswell Collins, were related.

CHRISTOPHER FELDT

The Night Riders of Pickens County (Part 3)

The Life and Death of Policeman Lee Cape

Policeman Lee Cape had always suspected his enemies would eventually get him. But he would tell his friends, "But when they do, I'll be so old I won't have lost too many years anyway."

William Lee Cape, better known as Lee Cape, spent the better part of four decades in law enforcement. Lee was born two years before the Civil War began and by the age of 18, had moved in with his grandmother who lived in Pickens County.

Lee had a reputation by his early 20s for being a tough guy.

One of the earliest accounts of Lee's bravery was seen in 1885 when the Atlanta Constitution presented the following tale.

On one such adventure, Lee, 23, was described as being a very quiet, but utterly fearless young man, who had come north with an Internal Revenue Agent on the Marietta and North Georgia Railroad. Five moonshiners were approached by Cape and his party. They scattered and one ran by Cape and jumped into the icy waters of a nearby creek.

The following conversation ensued:

Cape: "Halt! Don't run." Lee pulled out a large revolver.

Moonshiner: (in the middle of the creek) "Hello Lee."

Cape: "Hello Mose. Come out and give up."

Mose: "Come out hell! You come in and take me if you want me!"

Cape: "You run and I'll shoot you."

Mose: "I won't run."

Cape: "Well, come out then!"

Mose: "I won't!"

Cape: "Well, stand there!"

Mose: "I'll do it!"

Cape: All right. You stand in that water and I'll stand here. I can stand it if you can."

Mose: (with teeth chattering) "Lee!"

Cape: "Hey?"

Mose: I'll have to cave, I'm coming out."

Cape: "All right."

Mose climbed out the icy water and dripping wet, and Lee led him off to camp.

The Vigilantes

A few years later, in 1889, Lee was listed as one of the upstanding citizens the Honest Man's Friend and Protector Group wanted to target. Lee was one of the officers who apprehended some of the original members of the group. He had a history of going up against moonshiners and they knew it.

One day, while he was arresting bootleggers at Aiken family Cemetery, (located on private property near today's Lumber Company Road, not far from the City Park) he got into a scuffle with a man named McFarland from Keithsburg, Cherokee County. McFarland was killed when a weapon Lee had confiscated accidentally discharged in a scuffle.

As a result, some people, especially moonshiners, thought Lee was too zealous in his pursuit of justice.

A Family Tragedy

The Haunted Cape residence in Hinton, GA

Then in 1924, tragedy struck. Levi, one of Cape's sons, showed up at Lee's home in Hinton and murdered Lee's other son Hobart. Levi went to prison for several years before finally being pardoned.

Hobert Cape was murdered by his drunk brother Levi

The Heinous Murder of Lee

In September 1927, Lee Cape was murdered in the line of duty while pursuing moonshiners.

He and his grandson had gone out for a drive on that Saturday afternoon, when at approximately 3 pm, Lee told his grandson to leave him and return an hour later. At around 4 pm, Lee's grandson heard five shots in the direction his Lee had gone. When his grandfather never returned, the grandson traveled to Jasper and reported it to the local authorities.

That afternoon, Lee followed a group of men to the house of Carter Wilson. When Lee told the men he was going to inspect Hoyt Evans' coupe. Lindsey replied, "We'll see about that." Lee retorted. "No one's afraid." And began searching the car. Cape's last words were uttered.

Lindsey shot 65-year-old Lee in the head and then twice more after he fell. He loaded Lee in the back of Hoyt's car and drove his lifeless body some 40 miles away on a rarely used road a few miles from Adairsville. Lindsey was gone most of the night disposing of the body before returning home.

Lee's naked and decapitated body was discovered two days later by Rex Sherman while hunting rabbits. Lee's head was found 300 yards away on the opposite side of the street.

The Funeral

On September 20th, William Lee Cape's funeral in Hinton was the largest ever attended in the history of Pickens County. His casket was open so onlookers could see his body, although his head was covered. Sheriffs from Bartow, Gordon, and Cobb counties were present as were many other law enforcement personnel, friends, and family. Colonel Sam Tate spoke in praise of the illustrious lawman, proclaiming Lee to be "one of the staunchest enforcers of the law his county ever had."

The Epitaph on Lee's tombstone reads,

THROUGH THE PERFORMANCE OF HIS DUTY IN THE ENFORCEMENT OF LAW HE SACRIFICED HIS LIFE

The Trials

Six people were wanted in connection with the murder. Lindsey Evans, Walter Gradon "Grady" Evans, Hoyt Evans, Mrs. Evans, Carter Wilson, and C.L. Smith. There were several trials in Pickens County. Hoyt and C.L. Smith were sentenced to life in prison. Walter Evans was found not to have been involved. The other two men were sentenced to being an accessory to murder and served a year on the chain gang.

The Aftermath

- Hoyt Evans escaped from prison and made his way to Arkansas before being caught and sent back. He was pardoned in 1941.
- Lindsey W. Evans was never caught and by the 1940's it was assumed he was dead.
- Lindsey disappears from census data and all other government records after 1920.
- Two years before Lee Cape's murder, Lindsey had a child with Alice Chambers. The record of their marriage has been lost although Alice's 1930 census form shows her as being married and living with her five-year-old son Hicks Milton Evans.
- Alice and Hoyt remained in Fairmount after the departure of her husband, and her 1940 census shows her marital status as widowed.

NOTE: In searching through Hoyt's records, a Social Security Claim he filed as an adult names Lindsey William Evans as his father.

Mystery Man

Meanwhile, in 1930, in California's San Bernadino County, a man named Lewis Milton Coleman appeared out of nowhere. There are very few records that belong to Lewis M. Coleman, and none of them exist before 1930. Coleman's census records start right where Lindsay William Evans' records stop. Lindsey's last census record was the census of 1920.

He worked at a service station in Devore where he stabbed someone. Later he began working for the Santa Fe Railroad as a boiler repairman.

Another Clue

Coleman's Social Security number was 708-09-7116, a number issued only to railroad workers between 1936 and 1951. His social was not issued in Georgia. It was issued by the Santa Fe Railroad where he was employed.

Lindsey William Evans Revealed

- On Hicks M. Evans' Find a Grave profile, Lewis M. Coleman is listed as his father. Lewis Milton Coleman.
- The Lewis Milton choice of names was inspired by Lindsey William Evans' father's name, Milton Lewis Evans. He merely reversed the middle and first name of his father.
- Lindsey, under the alias of Lewis M. Coleman, lived out the rest of his days in California, got married, and had two children, a boy, and a girl.

Milton Lewis Evans - Lindsey/Lewis Milton's father

Lewis Milton Coleman

Lindsey William Evans was born on May 1, 1899

Lewis Milton Coleman was born on May 1, 1903

They died together on October 10, 1982

Note: Lewis M. Coleman made the news in San Bernadino in 1933 for stabbing Frank E. Medock of Glen Helen, CA at Coleman's Service station in Devore, CA.

Note: In an odd twist of events, William Lee Cape and the son of his murderer, Hicks Milton Evans, share the same June 5th birthday.

The Night Riders of Pickens County (Part 4)

The Other Fugitive

C.L. "Seal" Smith aka Carter Lee Smith

As with Lindsey Williams Evans, Carter Lee Smith, C.L. "Seal" (a pronunciation of the C and L together) Smith, was determined not to spend a life in jail. He was convicted and sentenced to life along with Hoyt Evans. Carter Wilson and Carter Jones were sentenced to 12 months of hard labor.

Like Lindsey Evans and his wife, Carter, and Rosetta Harriet Matilda Rosetta Smith, nee McCollum, gave birth to a daughter about two weeks before Cape was murdered. Once incarcerated, C.L. worked in several labor camps in Jackson, Cobb, Muscogee, Cherokee, and Whitfield Counties.

As a point of interest, Carter's wife moved to Whitfield County around the same time he was in a camp there. Then in January of 1931, C.L. escaped a labor camp in Cherokee County. He was never recaptured.

In the 1930 census, Carter's wife was listed as being married. In the 1940 census, she was listed as being single. Her daughter Estell married and moved away. In 1947, Carter met with his niece Pansy and her future husband at a movie theatre in Oklahoma. After, he took a bus to Arizona. This was the last time he saw any of his family.

Carter Smith was found dead on July 31, 1957. His body was behind a mattress factory in Casa Grande, Arizona. The Sheriff's Department found identification on him. They knew his name and age. However, they had no idea of who his kin were, or how long he'd been in Arizona as had no address in the state. His social security number had been assigned in Arizona between 1936 and 1950. The same period that Lindsey Evans had his California SSN assigned to him.

Carter Lee was buried in Mountain View Cemetery, in Pinal County, Arizona among another 140,000 plus others.

Mountain View Cemetery - Casa Grande, Arizona

Connahaynee

Mountains, sky, field and rocks

Timbers and nails, woolen socks

Paths and trails, blazes on trees

guests reveled in nature's breeze.

Darkness fell, an early night

Barn owls called to hunt at night

Bears retreated, asleep 'til spring

Scarce to eat, no wasted thing

Valley, dale, spur and draw

Snowflakes whirled until the thaw

Then fires roared beside the brick

Too hot to handle and spread too quick

Chestnut logs burned that night

The guests all fled in urgent flight

The Colonel's dream was now no more

The Lodge burned down unto the floor

Mountains, sky, field and doom

A vaulted chimney upon a tomb

CHRISTOPHER FELDT

The fires are gone, but the past won't stop

beneath the trees of Burrell Top

The Depression Era

The Whittington House and the End of the Dude Ranch

Starting with the second woman to the right, Mrs. Whittington, Emily, Charles, and Gladys

Was this house the Whittington home/GladJoe Inn? It certainly was part of the Dude Ranch/CCC Headquarters

Immediately, trees were harvested from the mountain area and work began on a large house. One that held a 1,600-square-foot living room with a fireplace that could easily hold an eight-foot log. Apart from being large and filled with conveniences, water was piped in directly from a gravity-fed mountain stream. A thirty-gallon water heater provided hot water and gas lanterns provided the lights.

A building directly across the driveway was made as guest quarters and was named Twin Oaks. In 1917 Charles was conscripted into the First World War. His wife and two daughters stayed behind to live in the palatial mountain residence. Up until the early 20s, the house had doubled as a summer hotel known as the GladJoe Inn. GladJoe took its name from the two Whittington daughters, Gladys, and Emily Josephine.

Gladys Whittington

Mrs. Glee Brock Thompson, who recently moved to Charlotte, N. C., to make her future home. Mrs. Thompson was formerly Miss Emily Josephine Whittington, attractive daughter of Mr. and Mrs. Charles W. Whittington.

Unfortunately, a cholera outbreak and mountain lions decimated his livestock, and his dreams were dashed. When Charles got back from the war, they moved, and the home was eventually purchased by Sam Tate via the Georgia Marble Company.

In 1929, during the beginning of the Great Depression, Colonel Tate opened his 10,000-acre Tate Mountain Estates. It had a private lake, mountain lodge/hotel, Dude Ranch, and much more. It was the premier summer resort for Wealthy Atlantans.

The Dude Ranch was visited by people from all over the Southeastern United States in search of rugged horseback adventures. It was run by the enigmatic Blink Drummond, an amazing woman who was a champion equestrian, trick rider, and pistoleer.

A few years later, Col. Sam decided to house a Civilian Conservation Corps Camp at the Whittington property. Camp 1449/P-77 was opened in 1933. Two-thirds of the 200 men from the camp lived in two rows of tents between the barn and the mansion. One-third of the men lived in the loft of the barn.

The Twin Oaks served as quarters for the few military officers of the camp and Sam Tate's surveyor, E.C. Perrow (father of Doctor Guerrant Perrow and grandfather of BT resident Janet Vardaman) lived in a nearby cabin.

The men built a dining hall and a recreation center that doubled as a dance hall once a month. They would routinely go to Marble City (Now Marble Hill) to pick up women to dance with and musicians for live music) The men dynamited roads up Hendrix Mountain to Mount Oglethorpe and helped to build roads up Burnt Mountain. (some of their work may still be seen as retaining walls along one of our evacuation routes) For their education, Camp Superintendent Perrow would teach them mathematics, physics, mechanical engineering,

French, and other classes. (Mr. Perrow was a Harvard graduate as well as a noted historian of American folksongs) By 1934 the camp had relocated to Butler County and had left their mark in road construction and buildings. In 1935, the Georgia Marble Company advertised a reward for arson that had damaged the area of the Dude Ranch.

In 1937, a few members of the Georgia Appalachian Trail Club, including Maurice Abercrombie, carried the sign designating the Southern Terminus of the Appalachian Trail up from the Dude Ranch site.

Over the next two decades, a series of renters occupied the property. The Darnells, Milfords (who used the CCC mess hall as a dance hall), Waters, and Evans families all lived at the property until December 24th, 1951. On that day, a fire swept over the property and the barracks that doubled as a chicken house was destroyed.

Lillie Mae Pendley remembers her father Vernie and other residents tried putting out the fires, but it all happened too fast.

Tate Mountain Estates

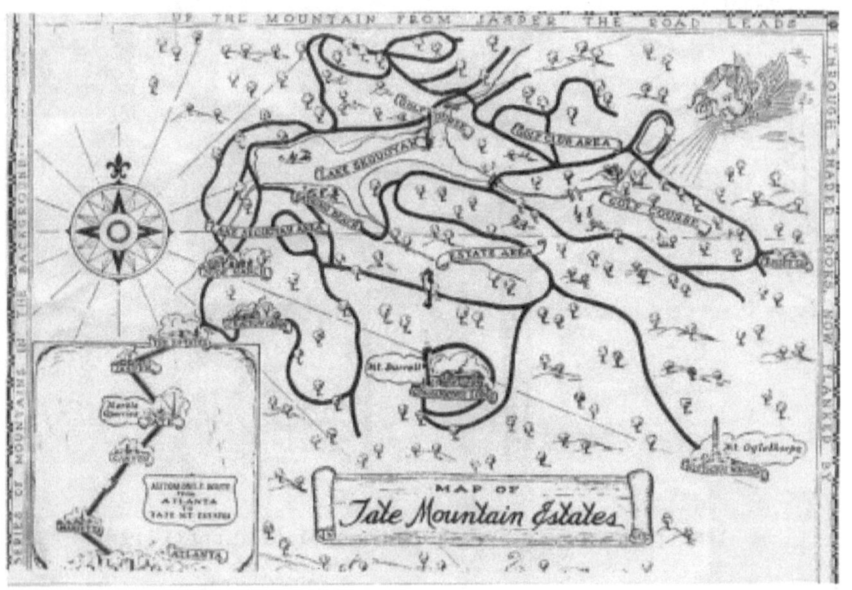

Map from an early Tate Mountain Estates Publication (early 30s)

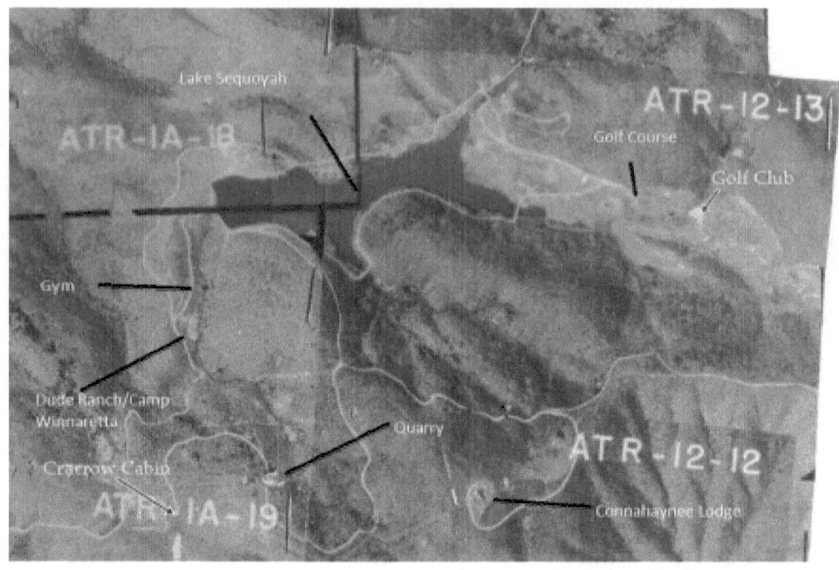

Aerial photograph of the area with notable locations (1949)

In 1930 Colonel Sam Tate had a vision. He would buy 10,000 acres and build a summer colony in a valley nestled near the Appalachian Mountains. The Appalachian Trail's southern terminus would suit just a few miles away on top of the mountain he successfully petitioned the state of Georgia to rename. He built a 51-acre lake and named it after the great Cherokee teacher, Sequoyah. He built an 18-hole golf course and Dude Ranch. His crowning achievement was the magnificent Connahaynee Lodge set atop Mt. Burrell. The lodge was made of stone, chestnut logs, and marble. It had 30 rooms with marble bathrooms. There was a giant guest room with a massive fireplace. The lodge was so massive that it could be easily seen from over ten miles away from Amicalola Falls.

Colonel Sam sold the estates before he died in 1938. In 1946 his beautiful lodge burned to the ground on a cold spring night.

Today there are still some thirty-odd homes surrounding Lake Sequoyah. The lodge ruins rest atop Burnt Mountain, and its one remaining chimney stands some forty feet tall, just barely beneath the canopies of the seventy-year-old trees that surround it.

The original plans from the golf course architect Van Kleek

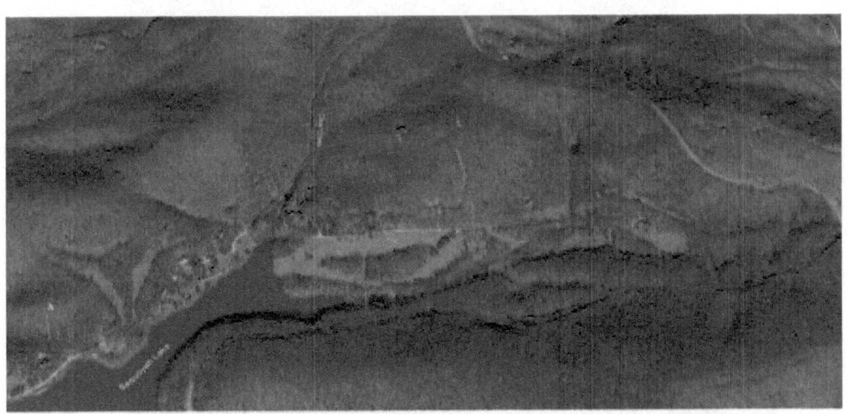

The 18-hole golf course is no more, but still can be seen

from satellite imagery quite easily

Bridge over Lake Sequoyah from the former golf course

The quarry from where the roads for the Tate Mountain Estates were made has been inoperable for decades

Fritz Orr Gym

The ghosts of the 1930s haunt us still. The old gym stands abandoned. This property still has the name Fritz-Orr in its legal description. Fritz-Orr ran a summer camp called Camp Tate here for about two years in the late 30's. This was near the second Dude Ranch location.

A postcard showing the interior and exterior of the Connahaynee

Lodge, and Lake Sequoyah

Bedroom at the lodge

Dining Room at the lodge

CHRISTOPHER FELDT

Sports Room at the lodge

Hall at the lodge

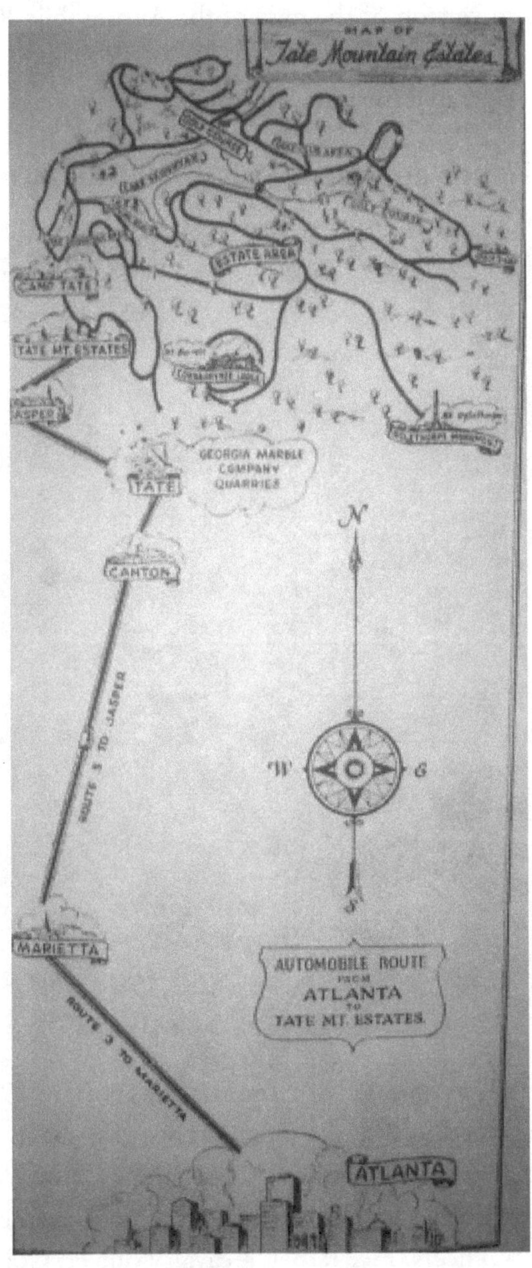
MAP OF
Tate Mountain Estates
ESTATE AREA
TATE MT. ESTATES
JASPER
GEORGIA MARBLE
COMPANY
QUARRIES
TATE
CANTON
N
W   E
S
ROUTE 5 TO JASPER
MARIETTA
ROUTE 3 TO MARIETTA
AUTOMOBILE ROUTE
FROM
ATLANTA
TO
TATE MT. ESTATES
ATLANTA

A more modern version of the map of the Automobile Route to Tate Mountain Estates from Atlanta. Camp Tate (The Second Dude Ranch location) only operated for a few years in the late 30s.

The Dude Ranch and the Inimitable Blink Drummond

Elizabeth Blink Drummond (nee Thomas) was born in 1906 while her family was stationed in Manilla. Her parents thought it cute that she had a habit of always blinking her eyes, so they gave her the nickname Blink. It stuck with her for the rest of her life. Blink came from a long line of military officers. Her father, a cavalry officer, Colonel Charles Oscar Thomas, Jr. was born in 1871. His father before him, was born in 1838 in New York State and fought for the Union in a regiment in Michigan.

From an early age, Blink showed a propensity for athleticism, leadership, and horsemanship. As a teenager, while living in La Jolla, California, Blink became one of the first girls in the country (1917) to win the Golden Eaglet Award, the highest award given to the Girl Scouts. As her father and grandfather knew before her, a life of pleasure was a mounted one. Her father's equestrian example left a lifelong impression on Blink, one that would later define her in many respects. She was known in La Jolla as being their most daring horsewoman.

In her early 20's, Blink, as an up-and-coming debutante, graduated from the prestigious Pomona University in California, shortly before the family relocated to Texas. In Texas, we see the first competitive evidence of Blink's outstanding horsemanship. In an Army event held in San Antonio, she tied for first place after competing against 28 of the military's finest mounted entries. This would be the first of her many equestrian awards. In 1923, she competed against 400 other riders in a massive equestrian event held at Fort Sheridan, Illinois. Once again, Blink took first place.

After a brief time living in Texas, she married native Texan Headrick Loran Drummond. Headrick's father William grew up in Hidalgo at the famous mission of Lomira. Regardless, after having a son, the relationship quickly ended and once again, she found herself living with her parents.

Blink's parents moved to Buckhead in the late 20's and shortly after Blink first came to live in Pickens County. Colonel Sam Tate's new development, the Tate Mountain Estates had a Dude Ranch. The Dude Ranch was one of a limited few located east of the Mississippi River. Blink and a fellow horseman, Laurence Beau Gay, were the main trail leaders of Col Tate's Dude Ranch. There were two Dude Ranch locations. The second Dude Ranch was named Triple C, after the location near the shore of Clear Creek on the west side of Lake Sequoyah.

Blink and Bo Gay at the 3C Ranch

The first Dude Ranch was built on the former property of Charles Whittington and was originally located on the present-day fairway of the sixth hole of Bent Tree Community, located near Jasper, Georgia. There were about 25 trail horses at the ranch. In addition to the stables, there was a kitchen, a dining hall, and a sleeping quarter for guests. There was also a giant farmhouse - the former Whittington house with a small guest building across the driveway known as the Twin Oaks.

Blink and Sharp Top Mountain as seen in early marketing material for Tate Mountain Estates

Riders would arrive from all over the southeastern United States to visit the ranch. From the ranch, they would ride up the mountain pass to the top of Mount Oglethorpe, and then head to Lake Sequoyah. From there, sometimes even by moonlight, they would take the horses as far as Amicalola Falls. Once a week Blink would take her horse down the dirt Jasper-Dawsonville Road to Jasper to check her mail and to get a coke. In most instances, Blink was known to be seen with her German shepherd Pal.

Blink is fourth from the front and is wearing a tie. Her German Shepherd Pal follows along

One of Blink's other duties was as the hostess of parties at the Connahaynee Lodge[1]. She had led socialite events like the Halloween Ball and others. Growing up in higher circles of the military had taught her these skills. Formerly she had led similar parties at Fort McPherson and other venues before she arrived at the ranch.

---

1. https://www.pickenspast.com/post/the-connahaynee-lodge-1930-1946

Connahaynee Lodge (1930-1946)

Sadly, as popular as the ranch was, Blink only stayed at the Dude Ranch for a couple of years before moving to Michigan. While there, Blink met a military man named Louis Gray. They had a whirlwind romance and traveled by cruise ship to the Hotel Gloria in Rio De Janeiro to get married. As her son got older, she taught him trick riding and other equestrian skills. Like his mother, grandfather, and great-grandfather, Peter was an amazing horseman.

Peter Gray standing on two moving horses

Blink moved yet again to Colorado. There she became the leader of a prestigious riding club in Denver known as the Hottentot Riding Club. Like the former Dude Ranch, the riding club had 30 horses for girls and boys between the ages of 8 and 18 to learn to ride.

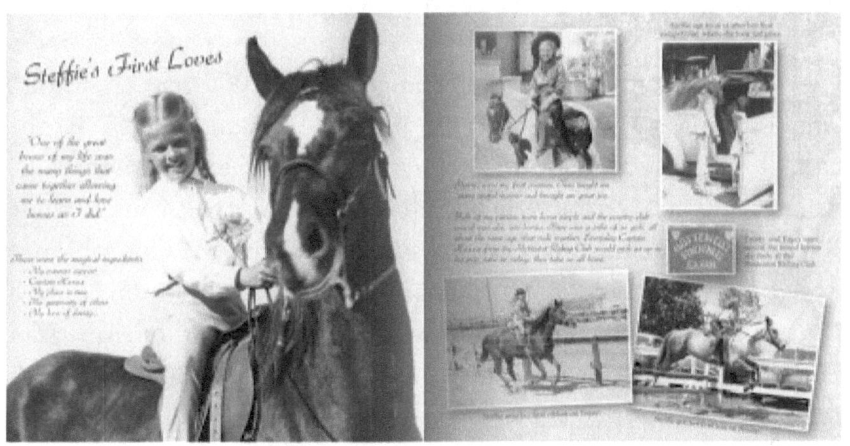

Picture of one of the countless Hottentot Riding Club members

In her later years, Blink sadly became bedridden and sickly. Her granddaughter Stephanie would listen to her tales of her younger years and exploits with a grain of salt. That was until I reached out to her with archival evidence of not only her times here in Pickens County but from all over the United States.

Other Adventures

One such tale, published in a newspaper in South Carolina, had detailed the time Blink had encountered an injured duck while traveling near Chatsworth, Georgia. She, being quite the expert at animal husbandry, decided she would take the duck with her to the hotel she was staying at in Knoxville, Tennessee. While there, she kept the bath half-full, so the duck had a place to wade. On that Sunday morning, the housekeeper, being completely unaware of the waterfowl guest, was astonished to find a duck in Blink's room. As it turned out, the duck was similarly astonished to hear a vacuum cleaner. The maid panicked and fled the hotel room screaming, only to be followed by the duck into the main lobby of the hotel!

The Connahaynee Lodge (1930-1946)

Col. Sam Tate announced the creation of a 10,000-acre estate that would serve as a summer resort for wealthy Atlantans in 1929. At the cost of one-million dollars (seventeen million in today's money) he would construct a 51-acre manmade lake, 18-hole golf course, Dude Ranch, and a premier place to rest and hold events, the Connahaynee Lodge. Situated some 3,300 feet above sea level, atop Mount Burrell (Burnt Mountain today), the giant lodge was built of American Chestnut Logs, local fieldstone, and marble. It held 30 rooms with marble baths, was two stories high, and had a great hall, dining room, parlor, basement, and more. At the entrance of the lodge was a circular gravel road that went around a putting green.

The Connahaynee Lodge

The living room lounge with fireplace and terrazzo floor

In 1930, when the lodge was built there were only two wings of the building. A few years later a third wing was added that gave the building the shape of a Y. The top of the mountain was mostly clear-cut, and visitors enjoyed a panoramic view of the area and its mountains. To the southeast one could see Mount Oglethorpe, Sharp Top Mountain further west, Jasper was visible to the south, and the rest of the Appalachian Mountain chain (and Lake Sequoyah in the winter) was visible to the north.

The living room pictured above had ceilings all the way to the top of the second level of the lodge, with a balcony and railings, bearskins and horns adorning the walls. The sofas were a deep red color, and there were armchairs for people to sit on, bridge tables, and more.

A postcard showing the exterior of the lodge, Lake Sequoyah,

and a larger rendering of the lounge room

Residents of Tate Mountain Estates and visitors would often come to the lodge on Saturday nights for beer (even though Pickens County was a dry county at the time), cigarettes, food, and entertainment. Other times there were balls and socialite events, fox hunting competitions, and equestrian events. For recreation, people could try their hand at archery or trapshooting, go swimming or boating in Lake Sequoyah, and play 18 holes of golf at the course. The Van Kleek-designed course was often attended by Charlie Yates and his friends. Bobby Jones even played a round once. In the early years, one of Col. Tate's people to host social events at the lodge was Blink Drummond (also the equestrian leader of Tate's Dude Ranch.) Various groups from Atlanta and elsewhere would hold events at the lodge, garden events, Halloween balls, etc.

The dining room of the lodge, apart from serving food, under Mr. Adams' ownership also had slot machines away in an adjacent alcove for people to play.

NOTE: Frequent visitors of the lodge, Frank Spratlin and family, would later play a major development role in Pickens County.

The lodge dining room with tables and chairs

Other entertainments offered inside the lodge were local bands, square dancing, a piano where musicians would play and sing requested songs, those written by Glenn Miller, Tommy Dorsey, and Artie Shaw, and more for the guests.

Then Tate Mountain Estates, Inc. filed for reorganization under the Bankruptcy Act in November of 1934. In 1935, the property was sold to the Appalachian Realty Company. By 1940, after suffering financial hardships, the lodge was sold again to Joe Adams, former owner of the El Comodoro Hotel in Miami, Florida. Joe got into a dispute over which rights to the use of the estates, including the lake, were conferred to him in the sale of the land. Years later, the rights were settled.

In March of 1946, the caretaker, Fuller Forrest, noticed some electrical wires that were too hot. A fire had started in the basement and spread to the kitchen. He ran off to get help, and by the time help arrived the lodge was engulfed in flames. Given the topography, remoteness from water, and fire departments from Jasper, despite everyone's best efforts the lodge was destroyed.

Fire destroyed the lodge March 1946

Somehow, despite it all, several chairs were salvaged from the dining room of the lodge and taken to a residence in Grandview Lake.

One of those chairs sits in my office today.

One of two chairs from the lodge in my collection

Some years later, Frank Spratlin, a member of the board of regents from
WGST agreed to put a radio tower near the former site of the lodge.

Today, the remains of the lodge are still in the forest, a solemn reminder
of a different era, complete with most of the fieldstone and a large,
still-standing chimney.

The lodge in the early 30s

Civilian Conservation Corps

Camp 1449 / P-77 (1933-1934)

The Great Depression of 1929 caused massive hardships across the United States of America. In response to the dire economic situation, President Franklin Delano Roosevelt created a series of public works programs designed to employ thousands of Americans in different areas of infrastructure, agriculture, and forestry-related jobs. For nine years, the Civilian Conservation Corps changed the American landscape by building fire towers, fire brakes, roads, and planting trees. By the summer of 1942, the men from the C.C.C. had planted a staggering 3 billion trees across our country. Over that same period, there had been over 78,000 men employed across a total of 127 C.C.C. camps in Georgia. (30-35 camps were operating at any one time)

In June of 1933, a Civilian Conservation Corps camp was built on Colonel Sam Tate's 10,000-acre Tate Mountain Estates. It was built on the site of Tate's former Dude Ranch - where for over a year people who visited the Tate Mountain Estates would embark on horseback rides, sometimes traveling as far away as Amicalola Falls some eleven miles away. According to the Pickens County Progress, the ranch house and other buildings made it a good location to start. (**NOTE**: The Dude Ranch was built by Vernie Champion around 1911 for Charles H. Whittington, an early land developer. To learn more about the origin of the Dude Ranch. It was also the first camp in the state to get started on its forestry work. The primary reason for its early start was because of its leadership. The Camp Superintendent, Eber Carle Perrow, had already surveyed the vast majority Col. Tate's lands and knew the mountains and forests of his estates intimately.

The old dude ranch house served as the Headquarters Building for the year the camp was there. Note the ambulance in front

The officers of Camp 1449 and a better shot showing the size of the ranch house

Captain W.M. Bomer, 1st Lieutenant Floyd L. Brown, 2nd Lieutenant Harold Gourgues (first-row center) along with the civilian staff (The Camp Inspection report from Dec 2, 1933, lists H. V. Brinkman, W.F. Montgomery Jr., M.J. Montgomery, F.W. Neel, J.D. Adams, Gordon Maddox, W.H. Johnson, Fred Forbes, Don Wallace, M.P. Dean, R.F. Conn, C.H. Keys, and a medical officer named 1st Lieutenant H.J. Bradley

For just under a year Camp Langley - named after a deceased C.C.C. man who died in training at Fort Benning, built roads within Tate Mountain Estates (including the main road up Hendrix and Big Stump Mountains, and several others, including a road that ran from Big Stump Mountain to Lake Sconti on the eastern side of Mount Oglethorpe. They also made the fire tower on Sassafras Mountain, near the area around present-day Monument Road, and built various fire breaks to prevent the spread of fires. One of the fire brakes is still reportedly visible as a small trench that runs quite a distance on a hilltop just south of Bent Tree's southeastern border, not far from a fork in Darnell Creek. According to 1st Lieutenant F.L. Brown, the base camp location was built at around 2,400 feet elevation. This elevation marker is far different than the elevation of the primary camp location located at 1,600 feet.

At the camp, two-thirds of the men lived in two rows of tents, six men a piece, between the barn and the ranch house that served as Headquarters. The remainder of the men lived in the loft of the barn. The officers lived in the Twin Oaks, a former guest house of the Old Whittington Dude Ranch. There was also a forestry office and a field kitchen.

One-third of the camp men lived in the loft of the barn and all of them took showers on the ground level

Two of the makeshift structures on the left are a barber shop and a clinic. One of the remaining structures was a canteen where the men could buy supplies. There was a barracks that doubled as a kitchen too. The Army mess officer in charge of the kitchen, 2nd Lieutenant Harold W. Gourges, was a native Louisianian. After his years in the CCC, like other men at the camp, went on to serve in World War II. According to Thomas Faircloth, another enrollee at the camp, the men who worked in the kitchen were treated like kings just like the men who cooked in the days of the wagon train.

The kitchen staff at the camp

When the men weren't engaged in Forestry work, they had ample time to learn various subjects that were taught at the camp. Among the classes offered, there was: Reading, Writing, French, business math, civics, engineering, sociology, history, mechanics, forestry, and more.

Professor E.C. Perrow (seen much later at his private mailbox house near Ball Creek) was the Camp Supervisor and Educational Instructor

The men engaged in various recreational activities like horseshoes and basketball and attended church services at the camp every two weeks.

Camp 1449 - P-77's Basketball team with David Louis Hardegree at the far left, second row

Once a month the men would hold a monthly dance and go into Tate, Marble City, and Jasper to find dance partners. Sometimes local schools would hold box-suppers - a practice where a man would not only win a fully prepared meal but also gain a date with the lady who made the meal. One of the young ladies who lived closest to the camp would routinely sneak out with the men. This would only happen when her younger sister would take a quarter as payment for arranging the tryst. By 1934, the younger sibling had earned a solid twenty dollars of quarters.

All in all, there were about 200 men at the camp. Three of the men were Army officers. Thirteen of the men weren't enrolled in the CCC and held jobs as foremen, machine operators, blacksmiths, and camp supervisors. 176 men were assigned to forestry work.

Some of the unidentified men in the following pictures were George "Lumberhead" Cannon, Richard "Baby Ray" Kimberly, "Penrod" Peavy, Henry "Dr. Foots" Jordan, Thomas Faircloth, Frank Bullington, Darden, Deese, and McDaniel

Originally the men at Camp 1449 were only supposed to stay for 6 months, but an extension was granted, permitting them to stay for a year. By June of 1934, many of the men had moved to CCC camp Butler in Taylor County. But for the most part, the men worked hard and served their country well.

They held a farewell ceremony in Butler, and the men looked back fondly on the time they had shared. Some men would move on to serve at Camp Bradley, F-7 in South Carolina, others would be discharged. All of them would think positively on their days in the forested mountains of Pickens County.

A year later, in 1935, there was a massive fire at the site caused by arsonists. By that time, the Georgia Marble Company had acquired the land where the CCC camp/Dude Ranch was. Georgia Marble offered a $250 reward in the Pickens Progress in December of 1935 to catch the person(s) responsible.

The fire took out over 2,500 acres and 30 men were called in to assist with putting it out. This fire was one of fourteen forest fires that happened that week. Nine of the fourteen were successfully put out right away. At times, the fire was being blown out 100 yards at a time with the high winds they had, and it was hard work to preserve some of the structures.

Reward

Will Pay $250.00 Reward for Information Leading to Arrest and Conviction of Party or Parties who set Fire to Woods on or Near Hendrix, Grassy Knob or other Mountains in That Range and Caused the Burning of Woods on These Mountains and Endangering Houses Located at old CCC Camp Site.

The Georgia Marble Co.

Tate, Ga.

A few years later in 1937, Georgia Appalachian Trail Club members carried up the original distance marker sign, three by four feet, to the top of Mount Oglethorpe in sections from the Old Dude Ranch

For seventeen years, the Appalachian Trail's original terminus was on the top of Mount Oglethorpe. The approach trail from Tate took hikers from the intersection of Highway 5 and Highway 53 east towards Marble Hill and eventually to the Dude Ranch as one of the waypoints to the start of the AT

From Ga. Highway 53, (0 m.) dirt road follows winding course. At crossroads, at 1.4 m., turn left downhill. At 2.7 m. is large walnut tree with double blazes and a road entering from left near a house. Beyond tree, turn right into dirt road. After passing house on left at 3.2 m., take left fork of road. Bear left on road between fields enclosed by rail fences and pass two houses with the name "Champion" on the mailboxes. At second house follow road right around barn and reach old "Dude Ranch" at 4.1 m. (The "Dude Ranch" is the site of a once

317   14-7

14-8   GUIDE TO SOUTHERN APPALACHIANS

flourishing ranch for guests of Tate Mountain Estates. A CCC camp was also once located here. The mountain home of the caretaker, Mr. Hendricks, is a few hundred feet from the approach road. Shelter is afforded in abandoned CCC building but no bunks or stoves are available. Consult caretaker when using building. From here to Mt. Oglethorpe the road may or may not be passable by automobile.)

Leaving "Dude Ranch", follow blue blazes past small building with sign "Twin Oaks" and continue along old road. Marble shaft on Mt. Oglethorpe may be seen frequently. At 6 m. is a small gap which is cultivated by Mr. Hendricks. Road continues along right of ridge beyond gap and, at 6.6 m., makes a sharp left turn with marked *spring* at right of road just beyond turn. This is a good reliable *spring*. Canteens should be filled as there is no water for 5.1 m. north of Mt. Oglethorpe. An old road from right enters at this turn. Approach road continues on from here and joins Appalachian Trail at 7.3 m. (The Appalachian Trail here is on the road from Connahaynee Lodge to Mt. Oglethorpe.) The summit of Mt. Oglethorpe is .3 m. to *right*.

Description of the approach trail from Tate with distances given

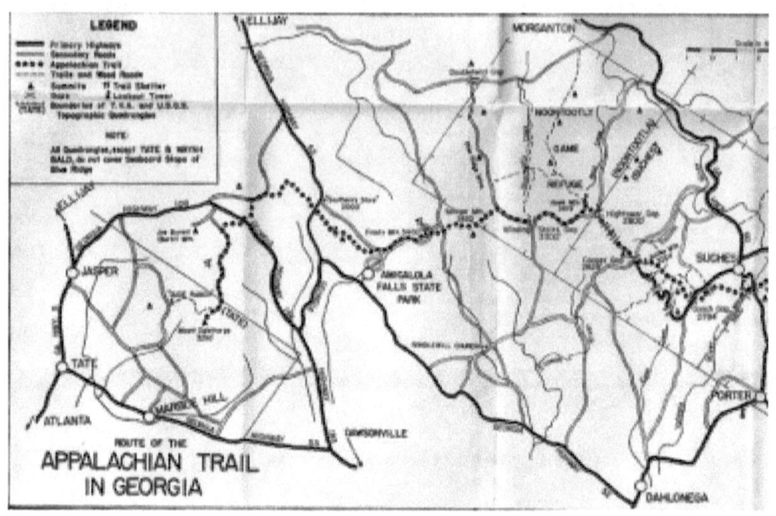

Original map from the 1942 Southern Guide to the

Appalachians - Dude Ranch just east of Mole Mountain

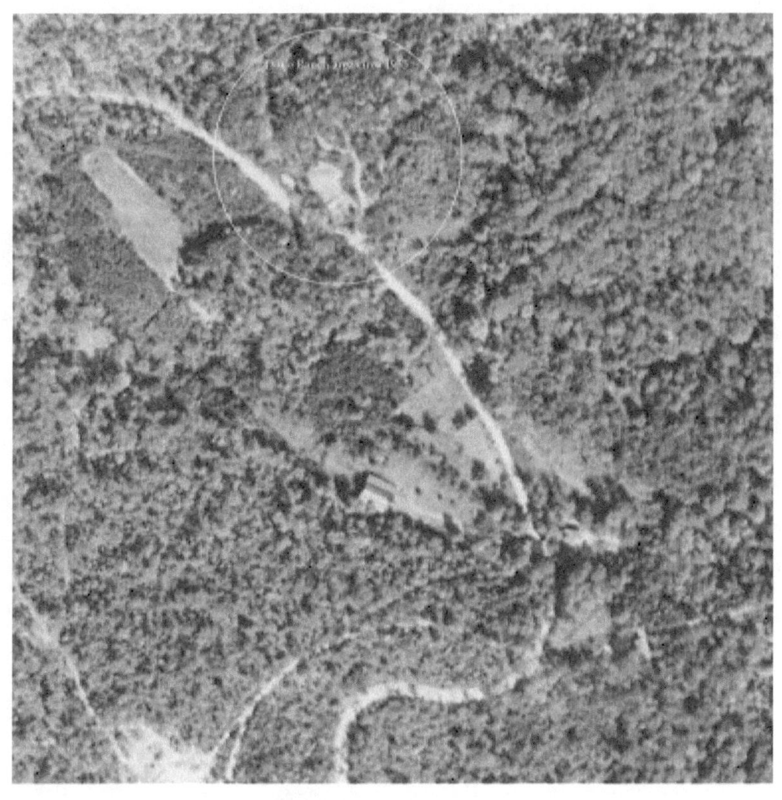

Dude Ranch area 1955

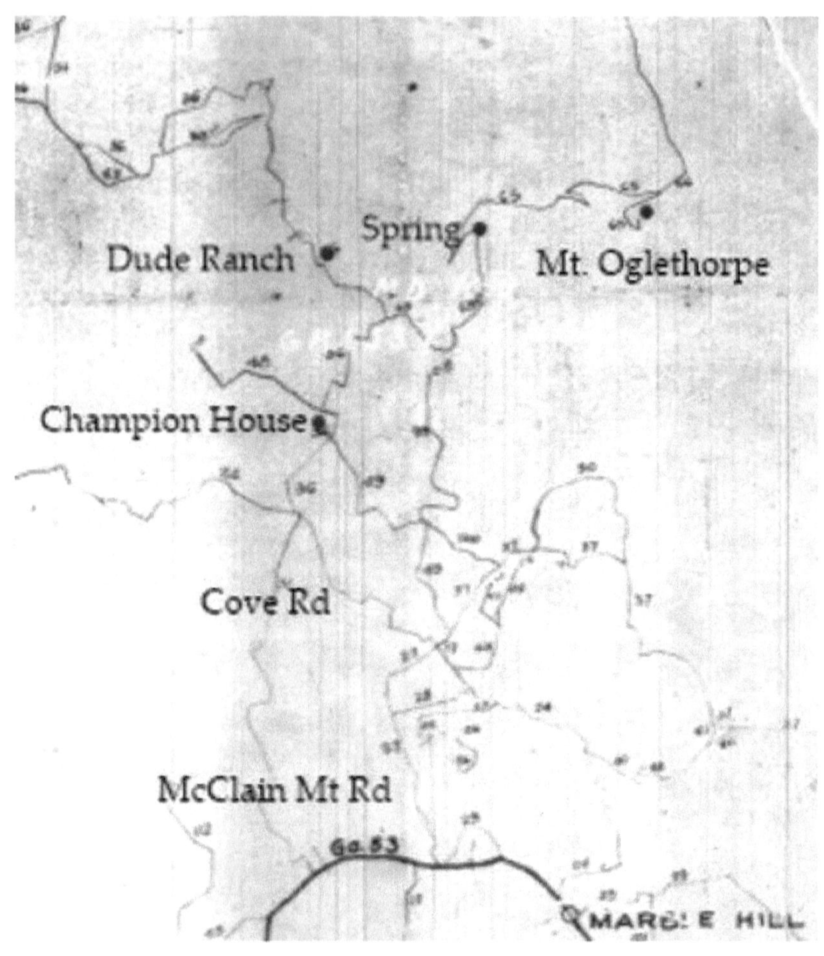

1940 Census Enumeration Map with locations

The location of former Camp 1449 as seen on Bent Tree Golf Course's sixth fairway

The Late Great Professor Perrow

"I went to the woods because I wished to live deliberately, to front only the essential facts of life, and see if I could not learn what it had to teach, and not, when I came to die, discover that I had not lived."

- Henry David Thoreau

Eber Carle Perrow, grandfather of Pickens County residents Janet Vardaman and Margo Austin, was born on December 7th, 1880, in Tye River, Virginia. When he was eight-years-old, he moved with his parents to Tennessee and quickly became fond of folk tales. A brilliant student, he became the class valedictorian of the class of 1903 at Duke University and graduated with a doctorate from Harvard University in 1908. Like J.R. Tolkien he was an able polymath (one who can speak fluently in several languages) and was easily able to complete his doctorate in Philology. Philology is the study of language in oral and written historical sources; it is the intersection of textual criticism, literary criticism, history, and linguistics. One of his philological observations about the influences of the railroad in developing our unique brand of language in Appalachia is excerpted below:

Railroads have forced their way through these regions, but their influences have touched the people only superficially — given them something to sing about, or possibly caused some of those living near the stations to take up the custom of wearing collars instead of the standard red handkerchief. The man back in the ridges, however, they have left unchanged."

Professor Perrow also chronicled American folksongs during early 20th century. His collection, Songs and Rhymes of the South is considered a landmark book on the subject matter.

Taken from it, his brilliant description of Appalachian people:

"Since their settlement in this region, there have been few enough influences brought to bear to keep this isolated people in line with the growth of the outside world. For a long time commerce left the territory unexploited: "What sholde it han avayled to werreye? Ther lay no profit, ther was no ridiesse." The rude log cabin of the mountaineer, with its stone-stick-and-mud chimney; the bit of truck garden near the house, tilled by the women-folk; the hillside, with its scant cover of Indian-corn, with now and then a creek-bottom in which weed and crop struggle on equal terms for the mastery; the cold, clear limestone water breaking from the foot of the ridges; the noisy trout stream, now clear as glass, now swollen by the almost daily thunderstorm; the bold knobs rising steep from the valleys and covered with blackberries or huckleberries; and in the background wave after wave of mountain forest, with its squirrel, wild geese,

'possum, coon, "painter," rattlesnakes, and an occasional bear, — these constituted the wealth of the country.

In 1910 he married Bertha Lillig, a former singer/concert pianist at the Met, in Boston, Massachusetts. Then in 1919 Professor Perrow, upon learning of his nervous indigestion from his physician, left his position at the University of Louisville teaching English literature and decided to move to his 500 acres of land that he had bought in Talking Rock. He arrived by train with his wife, two sons, a daughter, some cattle and his belongings.

His first few years in Talking Rock were arduous ones. Living off of a mere $15 dollars a month, he lived in a rickety old cabin. The leaky roof and the cold were challenging. The cabin at one time had a loft. The previous tenant had taken the lumber of the loft with him. According to Perrow, in those days, the cabin lumber was highly prized as it was the only lumber not nailed down in case you needed a coffin.

The land itself was formidable and difficult to cultivate. His neighbors, as few as there were, would come around once and a while and say something discouraging. Professor Perrow was keen on describing them as "prophets of evil", as they had nothing but doom and gloom to pass on.

However, over time and with much hard work, he was eventually able to build a much larger home consisting of eight rooms, a living room with a great chimney that would hold a six-foot log, and a sliding door to allow a truck through to deliver the log. There were many bookshelves built into the interior walls and naturally, they were all full.

At first, he had worked on his land and in 1924 became the surveyor of Pickens County. Eventually, he became Colonel Sam Tate's surveyor, working on the development that came to be known as Tate Mountain Estates. In what would become a lifelong trend, Professor Perrow built a cabin near his surveying site near Burnt Mountain. It was located on the south side of what would later be Highway 136.

Dr. K. C. Perrow, probably the only "county surveyor" in the South with a Harvard Ph. D., shown adjusting his expensive transit in the rough Pickens county hills. Photo Courtesy Atlanta Journal, J. H. Dilbeck, Photographer

Later in 1933, the professor became the Camp Superintendent of CCC (Civilian Conservation Corps) Camp 1449, P-77. He taught about 200 men from rural Georgia varying subjects like mathematics, French, English composition, history, sociology, civics, engineering, and forestry work. What a blessing that must have been for these men! To be paid to be taught by a Harvard graduate in the middle of the Great Depression!?

During his stay at the CCC camp (in the land that is now the sixth hole of Bent Tree Golf Course) he constructed a small cabin near the Twin Oaks building, a guest house of the former Whittington house (also the former location of the Dude Ranch – one of the only Dude Ranches located east of the Mississippi River.)

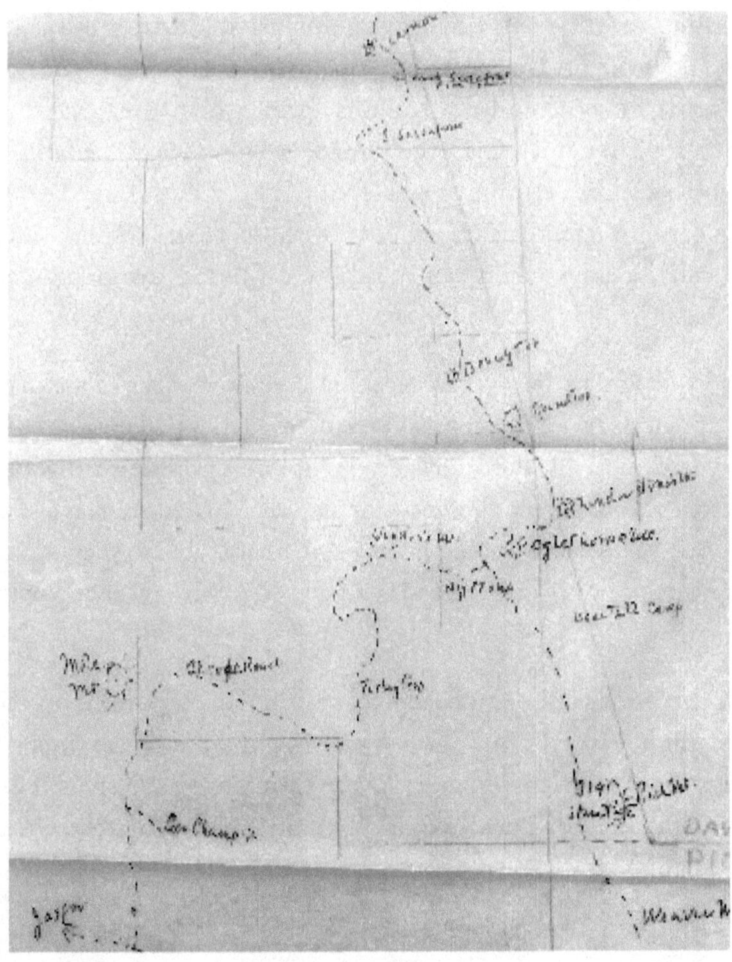

Perrow's hand drawn map showing the location of the Dude Ranch

According to Thomas Faircloth, one of his students, a camp medic named Henry Jordan (pronounced Jerdan) was part of the Jordan family, the force behind the Koinoia Farm, which later helped form Habitat for Humanity. Clarence Jordan, the founder of the farm had a writing shack like Perrow's (read more on the mailbox house later). His family farm in Americus was known by those closest to him to have a place where people could come and live off the land and learn about the Lord.

In 1953, Professor Perrow attended Duke University's Class of 1903 50th anniversary. Half a century before, as class valedictorian, he had been voted most likely to succeed by his peers. Undoubtedly, he had possessed the most unique life experience of his entire class. Having abandoned a career in academia long ago, he was able to share the trials and rewards of over three decades of rugged mountain living with his classmates.

In the professor's last decade, he led a regular Sunday afternoon class at Jasper Methodist after his Sunday morning discussions at Jasper First Baptist. He also continued surveying to earn money and spent leisurely hours in his mailbox house, a quirky and utilitarian structure, where he would light a small fire and write letters to his former colleagues and relatives.

One such letter to his niece Carolyn, written on Christmas Eve of 1963, a month after the assassination of President Kennedy, reflected on his life, his work and family:

"I guess it will be another quiet Christmas for me. The weather has been so cold for the last month I haven't been able to get over to Jasper often....I've done very little surveying this fall, and before long, I'll have to give up this work....but I'm thankful for such health as I have. You will write to me soon and tell me how Santa fared in the warm

Florida Sunshine. He still had on his Arctic boots when he passed there! Love to you all.

Uncle Eber

And finally, after reflecting upon his many years of living in North Georgia, he wrote the following words: (taken from his book Unto The Hills)

In my ... years in North Georgia, I have seen the "worser country" become the better. I have seen bare fields, once the unprotected target of winter rains, now covered with green pastures. I have seen the half-starved "outside" calf give place to fine registered cattle. I have seen forests once black with the ravage of fire now producing good timber and pulp. And I have seen almost impassable trailways become fair roads or even surfaced highways. We have today better schools with better teachers; our religious life, if not more deeply devotional, is, at least characterized by more of the greatest of the three virtues."

Professor Perrow passed away on December 20th, 1968, and is buried alongside his wife in Ball Creek Baptist Cemetery in Northwestern Pickens County. Before he died, the professor had built a final small shelter, equipped with his typical fireplace and bookshelves, with an adjoining room for a bed and table near downtown Jasper, located not too far behind First Baptist Church of Jasper. It still stands there today as the last accessible structure created by the late professor. It should be, like his words, preserved as a testament to a man – protean in his scope – a father, husband, friend, teacher, philosopher, surveyor, builder, scribe, and more. A man than not only read Thoreau, but a man who lived as Thoreau did.

What a blessing it was for a man of such immeasurable genius to settle in Pickens County – earnestly sharing his wisdom, grace, and knowledge with us for over half a century. What a blessing indeed.

Lament

Distant echoes,

voices skilled,

a funeral pyre of memories

Remembering desires

that Fate had stilled,

haunting, ethereal threnodies

Bowing towers,

steeples filled,

an orchestral mire of tragedies

beckoning clergy

that Time had chilled,

daunting, surreal reveries

Rustling branches,

zephyr willed,

a faceless procession of identities

laughing at all

that Death had killed,

unrelenting melodies

Part 5

Crime, Luck, and Redemption

Crime, Luck and Redemption: The Life and Times of Wallace Hughes, Jr.

Pickens County has a history replete with convicts who escaped local authorities. This story took place near Sharptop Church (near the present-day corner of Grandview and Pendley Road) and moved to the Connahaynee Lodge grounds within Tate Mountain Estates before the convict escaped our county.

On September 2, 1937, a group of convicts were near Sharptop Church, when one of the convicts, a man convicted of murder, escaped from the group, and ran up an embankment. A flurry of bullets was released, and the man stumbled. When the deputies ran to where the man fell, they were surprised at the lack of blood in the area. Wallace Hughes was not wounded, nor did he stay around for any length of time. A posse of 50 men with bloodhounds searched in vain for a week without finding him.

Worried sick by the plight of her boy, Mrs. Lela Hughes Friday afternoon posed with Wallace Hughes, while a jury made up its verdict sending the youth to the death chair for murder. Staff photo by George Cornett.

Hughes had made his way to Burnt Mountain to the quarters of some servants of the Connahaynee Lodge. Reports differ as to whether Wallace acquired any clothes from the servants. Regardless, for the fourth time in Wallace's illustrious criminal career, he had escaped. After escaping North Georgia Wallace made his way to California, New York, and Chicago before returning to Atlanta.

Wallace's criminal career began in 1932, when at the age of 17, he killed two men while holding up a restaurant in Atlanta. He fled the restaurant being chased by police. Gunshots were exchanged as Wallace made his way across several rooftops of buildings in downtown Atlanta before finally being captured atop the Georgia Power Company building. He was arrested and sent to trial. After taking his own defense, the presiding judge had sentenced Wallace to death by electric chair.

Wallace Hughes, Jr. was born in Fulton County, Georgia in 1915. He lived with his mother and father, and two older sisters. During the trial, he testified that his father Wallace Hughes, Sr. had introduced alcohol to him as a child and had eventually deserted the family. He claimed that the effects of his childhood had led him to a life of crime.

A year later, feeling pity on the youthful Wallace, Governor Talmadge had commuted his death sentence within seven hours of his execution. Yet Wallace decided that prison life was still not for him and decided to escape. In 1936, Hughes fled from a prisoner camp in Soperton, Georgia. This was his third escape.

Fast forward to January of 1938. After having been on the lam for 3 months, Wallace was recaptured by Atlanta police. The police had noticed a stolen car outside of a house on Beryl Avenue and searched the car. After securing two pistols, they raided the house. Hughes and three other criminals were arrested. Upon being arrested, Hughes was subsequently identified in a lineup for having robbed someone else between his escape and capture.

Wallace was sent to a prison farm at Reidsville, Georgia for a few years. However, in the spring of 1942, he and seven other prisoners orchestrated an escape. Three of the eight convicts were shot. Five of the eight were captured immediately. Wallace was neither shot nor captured right away. Later that summer, he was captured using the alias Buddy Hughes and charged with transporting a stolen automobile.

Miraculously and surprisingly, Wallace was allowed out of prison after having his life sentence commuted on November 11, 1956, and by 1958 he was living in Rome, Georgia, married and had taken up employment as an office machine repairman. Wallace outlived his wife and became a regular attendee of the Second Avenue Baptist Church of Rome. He passed away peacefully at the age of 64 in 1978.

Wallace lived most of his life as an outlaw, with blatant disregard for the property, life, or rights of others. And yet, time and time again, he consistently escaped justice, breaking free repeatedly and with amazing luck, avoiding gunfire in every case. In my research, I could not find record of his pardon from prison. After his death sentence was commuted to life without parole, barring a pardon, he should have never been released.

Regardless, his last decades were spent in marriage, work, and church as a contributing member of society. He found redemption.

Staged Death at the Cove

This is the tragic story of the Contreras family of Cherokee County, Georgia. In 1976, two teenagers killed their father and tried to make it look like an accident. For whatever reason, they decided the fictional site of the murder would be at the S-Curves below Cove Mountain, across the road from the entrance to the Perseverance Quarry.

In early 1976, Juan Contreras, Sr., and his wife Peggy divorced, and she and her daughter Vicki moved to Florida. When Peggy moved to Florida, her eldest daughter moved away from home, leaving behind three younger siblings, two boys, and a girl. Then in April of 1976, Peggy, committed suicide by shooting herself in the face with a shotgun. After her mom's death, Vicki quickly moved back to North Georgia.

On August 6, 1976, Juan and his sister Vicki planned to kill their father. When he arrived home from work, they bludgeoned him to death with a hammer. Panicked, they drove away in their father's red station wagon. While leaving they spotted the younger daughter's boyfriend, George Patterson. They stopped to talk, and the three of them left to dispose of the murder weapon. That night, Juan and Vicki stayed over at Patterson's. The following day, Vicki cashed her father's final payroll check. Later that night they went to a party and schemed of a way to cover up the murder.

21-year-old George Patterson of Ball Ground convinced 18-year-old Ronnie Lamar Moss from Jasper to help them dispose of the body. They drove Mr. Contreras' station wagon (with his lifeless body in the back seat) to the Cove located near the Perseverance Quarry two miles east of Jasper, siphoned gas from the tank, lit it on fire, and pushed it 200 feet down an embankment.

Ronnie Moss drove all of them back to the Contreras home where they gathered a bloody mattress, bedsprings, and rug, placed them in Moss's truck, and left to go burn the evidence. Subsequently, they cleaned the porch of the home and scrubbed the interior floors and walls down with ammonia.

Vicki Contreras 1976

They believed it would look like an accident. but made several mistakes. Their biggest blunder was leaving the severely burned body of their father in the back seat of the wagon. People don't drive from the backseat. The second was they pushed the vehicle over a cliff, instead of driving it. Under normal circumstances, a vehicle that crashes while traveling at a normal rate of speed will roll when going off an embankment. But the station wagon hadn't rolled or exploded.

Things seemed suspicious, prompting the investigators to order an autopsy. The autopsy revealed that Juan Contreras, Sr. had died from head trauma caused by three blows to the head by a hammer.

As a result, Juan Jr. and his sister were arrested and charged with murder. Further investigation showed that Vicki, then 18, had cashed her father's last payroll check from Lockheed and a motive. The teens were hoping to cash in on their father's $100,000 life insurance policy.

Ronnie Moss was charged with concealing a death and destroying evidence. George Patterson was charged with 3rd-degree arson, concealing a death, and destroying evidence. Juan Jr. and Vicki were charged with first-degree murder.

During the trial of the Contreras siblings, they both were found guilty and sentenced to life in prison. George Patterson turned evidence against them.

NOTE: One of the alleged motives from the Defense was that the crime was an act of revenge from Mr. Patterson against Mr. Contreras, Sr., who had a warrant issued for Patterson's involvement with Contreras' 14-year-old daughter.

In 1978, the Contreras siblings appealed their case to the Georgia Supreme Court arguing the lower courts had erred in their decision. However, the court denied their appeal.

A little more than a decade later, Juan Contreras, Jr. was paroled in 1988. His sister was paroled a year later. Juan (John) and Vicki Contreras quietly left the area and currently reside in Florida.

The National Forest Serial Killer, Huddle House, and the Dawsonville Wildlife Management Area

61-year-old Gary Michael Hilton, a.k.a. The National Forest Serial Killer finally got caught in 2008 after committing a grizzly series of murders. He had killed several people he had found while hiking in the National Forests of North Carolina, Georgia, and Florida. The entire scope of his murders is beyond what I'll cover in this entry. However, I will focus on the case of Meredith Emerson, due to its proximity to North Georgia.

TRAGEDY AND TRIUMPH: A NORTH GEORGIA HISTORY COMPENDIUM

Gary Michael Hilton in 2008

On New Year's Day, 2008, Gary Micheal Hilton was hiking in Blood Mountain, Georgia with his dog Dandy, when he saw 24-year-old Meredith Emerson hiking alone with her dog. He often used his dog to disarm the fear of his would-be victims. He began making small talk with her until he isolated and attempted to subdue her. She put up one hell of a fight, (she was extremely fit and had a martial arts background). Unfortunately, GMH won the battle and coerced Meredith into his van. At her request, GMH allowed Meredith's dog Ella to travel with her. In the van, he secured her and took her ATM card.

To buy time, Meredith repeatedly over several days gave GMH the wrong pin to her card. He attempted and failed to withdraw money from an ATM in Blairsville that evening. Two hours later, he tried again with no success at a bank in Gainesville. GMH's patience would only last so long. Later that night, GMH went to Regions Bank in Canton and entered the wrong PIN for the last time.

On January 3rd, he drove Meredith to Marble Hill, Georgia, and left her in the parking lot of the Huddle House while he went inside and called his former boss, John Tabor, asking him for money. The waitress Amanda Peacock, saw GHM drive away at around 5 pm. Unfortunately, John Tabor waited a few hours before notifying the authorities - losing what was likely the last chance the authorities would have had to find Meredith alive.

The Huddle House in Marble Hill where Hilton stopped to call his former boss while Meredith remained restrained in his van

The next day, GMH took Meredith to the forest of Dawsonville, near the site of the former Georgia Nuclear Aircraft Laboratory, tied her to a tree, and beat her to death with a tire iron. He dumped her body off an off-road trail in the WMA, decapitated her to remove the evidence, and left.

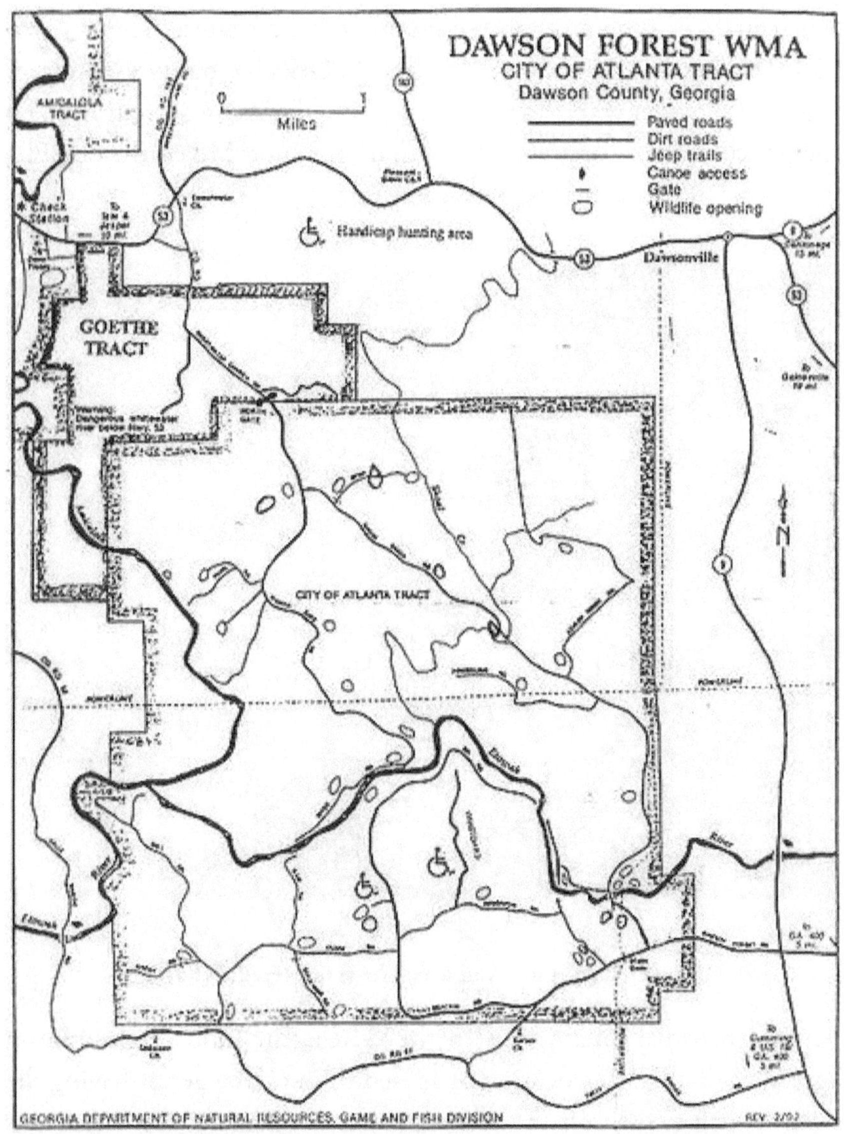

A map of the WMA where Emerson's body was found

On January 4th, he was spotted cleaning out his white Chevy Astro Van at a Chevron gas station parking lot in Dekalb County, Georgia. A vigilant bystander who had seen the reports of missing Meredith called the police and they apprehended him on the spot. Meredith's dog Ella was found nearby at a Kroger grocery store.

Hilton's Chevy Astro Van where he kept Meredith hostage

In an exhaustive interview with the GBI agent John Cagle, Hilton agreed to divulge the location of Meredith in exchange for having the death penalty taken off the table. On January 31st, 2008, GMH was sentenced to life in prison, with the opportunity of parole in 30 years, for the murder of Meredith Emerson.

Gary Michael Hilton is presently on death row at the Union Correctional Institution in Florida for the murder of Cheryl Dunlap.

GMH's Florida Dept. Corrections pic

The Griffeth Pendley Dogtrot Ax Murder

In 1877, a one-story dogtrot-style home was built off the old Dawsonville-Jasper Road (present-day Cove Road). Over the hill and south of the main east-west thoroughfare, the home sits in a field surrounded by woods. A dogtrot home has an open breezeway built between two sections of the enclosed house. This home was constructed of hewn logs, most likely oak. The dogtrot style of architecture was common in the late 19th Century and in many instances, these homes were used as post office locations for residents. Today, the house is only one of 156 in the National History Registry (out of some 82,000 total structures.)

The dogtrot passage is visible in this picture taken in 2008

Photo of the Griffeth Pendley home taken by the author in 2020

The land was sold in 1839 by the winner of the Land Lottery drawer for Land Lot 3, Section 4, William Perrett to Samuel Tate. In 1843, Samuel sold the land to his first cousin, Caleb Griffeth II (Both Tate and Griffeth families moved to Cherokee County in 1832 from the Lumpkin/Franklin County areas) By the 1860's the Griffeths had hundreds of acres of farmable land in Pickens County. Caleb, II passed away in 1868, and nine years later, his son Caleb Griffeth, III, built the first part of the dogtrot home in 1877.

Over the next few years, Caleb III built a well, a barn, and an outhouse on the property. His farming prospered and in 1905, he decided to build the Griffeth House (The former Jasper Junction on the corner of Grandview and Cove Road - where sadly, the Dollar General now sits) Contrary to popular belief, the former Griffeth home was not a trading post for the Cherokee Indians built in 1832.

The former Griffeth house was built in 1905 for a larger space for the Griffeth family to live in. Contrary to local legend, it never was a trading post. It wasn't located along the Federal Road nor built while the Cherokee were here

Thomas Monroe Pendley bought the property for $500 in 1905. Thomas, a former member of the notorious HMF&P (Honest Man's Friend and Protector) group - a vigilante group that in 1877 terrorized Pickens County and committed several arsons in battles against informants in the Moonshine Wars, was a former moonshiner and immediately planted two orchards on the property.

By 1935, Thomas had become one of the largest landowners in the Grassy Knob and Sharp Top Districts of Pickens County. After his death, the land was divided among his daughters. The Fann family held the land until approximately 1947 when they sold it back to Vernie Griffeth. They and their son Arnold Hoyt Griffeth rented the property and lived on it until the elder Griffeths died. In 1981, the property solely fell into the possession of Hoyt.

In 2008, the property was added to the National Register of Historic Places. Sadly, scandal befell the property. In 2014, Arnold Hoyt Griffith and Christopher Byers killed Ray Walnoha

by striking him in the head and neck with an axe. They then disposed of the body on the property and attempted to destroy the evidence. It was during this process that they burned down the barn.

It would be two years before Griffith was arrested for the murder. Rumors of Mr. Griffith being involved with murder had circulated since 2014, however, with no name or body, the sources were considered unreliable. Mr. Griffith was in jail in Pickens County when the charges were brought. Apparently, in a moment of bragging, he spilled too many beans. Griffith subsequently named an accomplice, Mr. Byers (who was in jail in Gordon County).

In 2018, Mr. Griffith pled guilty to attempting to hide the body (buried in the dirt on the Griffith property and hidden under sticks) and cleaning the murder scene. He admitted to bleaching the couch on the porch where the murder happened and the porch. However, it was deemed that he was not an active participant in the murder. Mr. Byers had later bragged that he came back to the property and moved the body to another location from where it would never be found. Some of the locations mentioned were the mine at the S-Curve off Cove Road (the old Perseverance Quarry), in a woodchipper across the street by the Community Gardens, the Edge of the World waterfalls on the Amicalola River near Juno, and or in a cave/hole near Grandview Lake.

Sadly, the interior of the dogtrot is no longer accessible due to contamination.

Arnold Hoyt Griffeth

(sentenced to one year)

Christopher Byers

(sentenced to life in prison)

Raymond Walnoha

(2014 victim of ax murder, body never recovered)

As an added bit of lore, Arnold Hoyt claims that the ghost of a slave woman that died on the property, before the construction of the dogtrot home, haunts the grounds of the Griffeth land.

The Unseen Conductor

The woods are vast, deep, and dark.

The wind blows hurriedly through the trees.

The branches respond with crackling bark -

in communion with the breeze.

The rocks are scattered upon the hills.

The mosses display their neon green.

The fallen leaves of arbors fill-

a hidden glen few have seen.

An Unseen Conductor (but not unheard)

connects each bridge to chorus.

And through the forest, the sacred words,

compose the song before us.

Part 6

Forgotten Places

Young Potts Cemetery

In 1829, a man named Young Potts moved to Dawson County from South Carolina. He hit the ground running and made a small fortune in his early prospecting in the late 1820s. Within a few years, to maintain anonymity, he and his family moved into the rugged terrain known as the Wolfscratch Wilderness in 1836. Located on LL 131 and 98, Young Potts purchased nearly 500 acres of land in the remote forests of Cherokee County.

Young Potts built his house near a spring and branch of Yellow Creek. Back in his time, his house was a sight to behold. It was a one-story, painted white, and featured a nice porch and paned glass windows. There also were a few outbuildings including a corn crib and barn.

The Potts house

He married in 1839 and had his first child in 1842. Within a few years, a family grave plot was established for his loved ones.

An old sign nailed to a tree indicates the direction of the plot

For those of you who are familiar with the territory east of Steve Tate Highway near Marble Hill, there is a Potts Mountain that takes the surname of Potts. And while on modern maps Potts Mountain refers to the mountain itself; in the 1800's it referred to a geographical region that was much broader than the mountain.

There is a legend regarding Young Potts and a slave of his. Potts and his slave traveled by horse to Atlanta to trade and sell items. In the 1800s the trip took about a week. On the return trip home, Young Potts was stirred from his sleep to discover his slave standing over him with an axe. Potts confronted him and the slave assured him that he wasn't trying to hurt him. Upon his arrival at his property, Young Potts quickly murdered his slave.

There is no gravestone in the family plot to indicate the location of the slave. However, there are about seven graves of Potts family members and their marriage partners and children.

In 1856, (three years and one day after the founding of Pickens County) Young Potts got sick and died at the age of 55.

Young Potts grave marker. (photo taken in 2022)

I discovered the location of the cemetery quite by accident. I was just about to give up looking during my first search when I found the wooden sign in the picture above. I found a second sign near a corner where two paths converge. This sign was weathered, and all the painted letters had worn off it. I brought it out of the woods to a friend and she repainted it. On my second outing to the cemetery, I nailed to the original tree it once hung from years ago.

Old directional marker, new paint

For those who would like to find the cemetery, I'll leave you a clue. It is at the D.W. Padgett marker on this map from 1903.

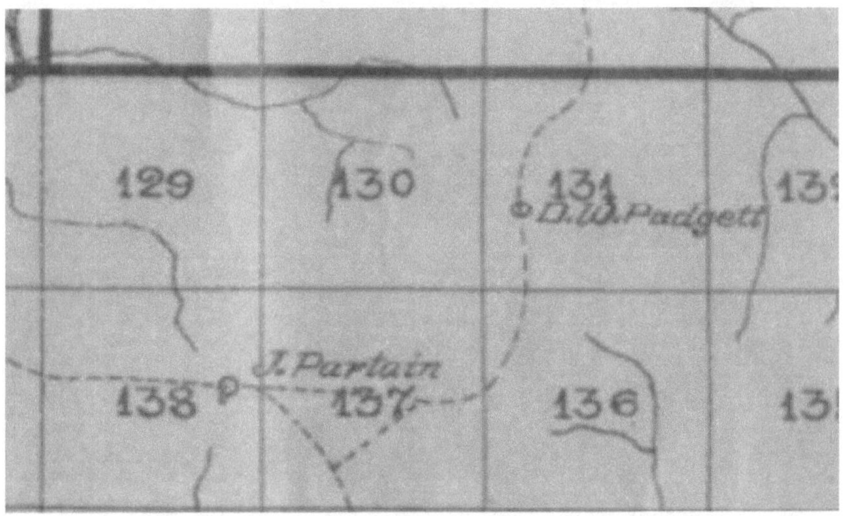

LL 131 on 1903 Henley Map

Lonesome City: The Forgotten Hamlet of Tate

According to Dr. Kathleen Thompson, in her October 5th, 2011, Pickens Progress article about Black Communities in Tate and Jasper:

"Lonesome City was located off Highway 53, across the road from the Tate House, and deep in the woods. Families living here predominately carried the last name Patrick. Reverend Bill Patrick was raised here. In the 1910s into the 1930s this was a Black settlement. By the 1950s this had become a White farming area. Due to job losses in the marble industry, Black families had moved away."

An earlier Pickens Progress article written in the 1970s by former teacher Carl Darnell had placed Lonesome City near Darnell Creek, south of Cove Road, near Marble Hill, not Tate. Darnell spoke of a story that spawned from reports of the deaths of several Cagle family members in the tornado outbreak of February 1884. However, newspaper reports from the Atlanta Constitution in 1884, indicated the deaths took place in Cagletown (near modern-day Hwy 108) in West Pickens County. Darnell recalled that someone found the bodies of the Cagle family the day after the storm, and from that moment on the area was known as Lonesome City. I suppose it's possible there were two such locations. However, the name of the town cannot be found on any local map.

However, there were a series of structures in the approximate location given by Dr. Thompson indicated on the Tate Nelson Quadrangle map of 1926.

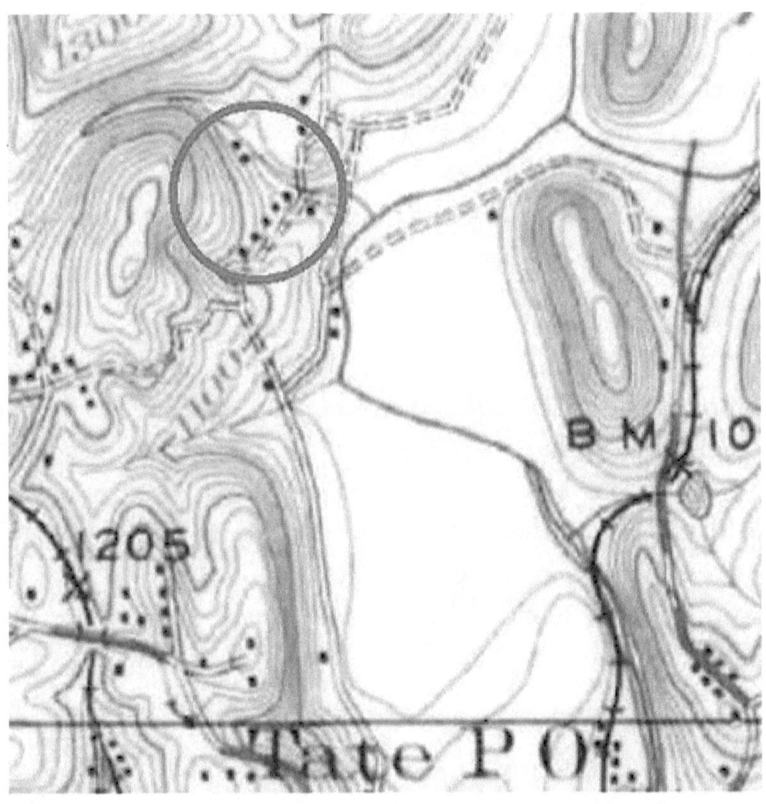

Approximately ten structures are indicated on the Nelson Quadrangle map

Between those sources and modern satellite imagery was able to discern an approximate latitude and longitude of the abandoned hamlet. Venturing out into the woods, I hiked along an abandoned roadbed that had washed out near the East Branch of Long Swamp Creek. I reached an open field and followed along until the path forked in two directions. I hiked in a southwesterly direction and climbed a hilly path that hooked to the south in the direction of Lonesome City.

It was at this moment that I stopped. I knew I was getting close. As I stared off into the woods a shape behind the trees emerged that was too angular to be natural. Thirty feet away, east of the trail was a giant marble chimney. A piece of the mantle had broken off. The opening of the hearth was at least three feet high and a foot deep. The chimney rose well above twenty feet into the sky. Each piece of the chimney was made of pristine blocks of white marble. Within a few yards of the chimney, a foundation was found. Among the debris, I located an aftermarket bucket lamp (a headlight modification to a car between the 20s and 50s.)

Further down the trail it dead-ended in a cul-de-sac. Downed trees blocked the road. And off again, to the east, I spotted a manmade structure. Off in the woods, I discovered a series of fallen chimneys and foundations. There were three total - four if you included the house with the marble chimney. Unlike the larger marble foundation, these homes were smaller and made from brick. To the left of the first delipidated home, I could see pillars that once held up a floor. And off to the right, I found the remains of a mostly intact 1953 Ford Customline.

Everything at the site supported the accuracy of the interviews conducted by Dr. Thompson. Lonesome City was lonesome, but at least for a few hours, welcomed my company.

The Old Coward/Fitts/Hendrix House

Standing not more than a mile away from Long Swamp Baptist Church is the old Coward' homestead. The Cowards had moved here (then Cherokee County) from Rutherford, North Carolina around 1840. On December 14th, 1843. James Coward, Jr. bought 160 acres of Land Lot 8, section Four of Cherokee County from Samuel Tate.

The house in 2021

The second incarnation of Long Swamp Baptist Church.

The original church was destroyed by a tornado in 1874

James later deeded one acre of LL8 to Long Swamp Baptist Church in 1858. Robert Cowart (also spelled Coward) sold the land to Hiram D. Cowart for $200. Hiram D. Cowart sold the land to Van Buren Tatum in 1874 and purchased it for $225.

Van Buren Tatum (center)

William E. Fitts bought the land in 1893 from Van Buren Tatum. William sold the land in 1941 to Henry Fitts. And Henry sold 80 acres to Ada Hendrix, Vida Hendrix, and Herman Hendrix in 1946.

Cicero and Ada Hendrix

Ada lived in the house with her daughter Vida and Vida's brother Herman until she died in 1971. Vida and her brother lived in Pickens County until the mid-90s. Since then, the property has changed hands about three times. While looking through the home, I found correspondence between former relatives of Vida Hendrix and shared it with their descendants. They were thrilled to have read it.

The Lost Town of Alice

Remains of the old Alice grist mill

Nowadays, if you were to drive down Salem Church Road, chances are you would have no idea that you were driving past a once-thriving community. However, up until the first decade of the 20th Century, Alice was an active community with a cotton mill, a grist mill, a sorghum syrup mill, a blacksmith shop, a one-room school, and houses.

The one-room school shortly before it collapsed

Alice was named after Tom Atherton's wife. Tom and his brothers, William and James moved to from Manchester, England to New Jersey, and then to Roswell, Georgia in 1840. They established the Roswell Cotton Mills, and in 1847, moved to Pickens County. In the 1860s he and his brothers built the Talking Rock Cotton Factory. The Atherton's opened a yarn factory the Shoal Creek Mill, in Waleska in Cherokee County, and finally in 1882 opened Harmony Mills in Alice.

William C. Atherton at his house in Alice

The grist mill in Alice was on the eastern side of Town Creek, just north of the waterfall. Nearby, within a few hundred yards was an operational gold mine. The brothers, Master of Engineering that they were, built a 500-foot-long wooden race to bring water to the mill site off the top of the nearby embankment. The water came from near Highway 515 where a small dam helped to channel the water.

The collapsed gold mine of Alice

Sadly, Harmony Mills was damaged by a flood and then destroyed by fire in 1897. By 1909, the post office was closed as most of the workers at the site had moved on.

R.J. Cox at his blacksmith shop in Alice

The site of Alice today

John Wesley Cagle and a Hamlet Named Jockey

In 1890, a small hamlet in south-central Pickens County named Jockey arose near the Cagle Mills on Sharp Mountain Creek. A post office was created in the same building as the local merchandise store, thereby designating Jockey as a 'post-hamlet.' An October 11, 1890, Pickens County Herald article detailed the creation.

The Postmaster of the newly appointed post office was John Wesley Cagle. He was appointed under the term of President Harrison.

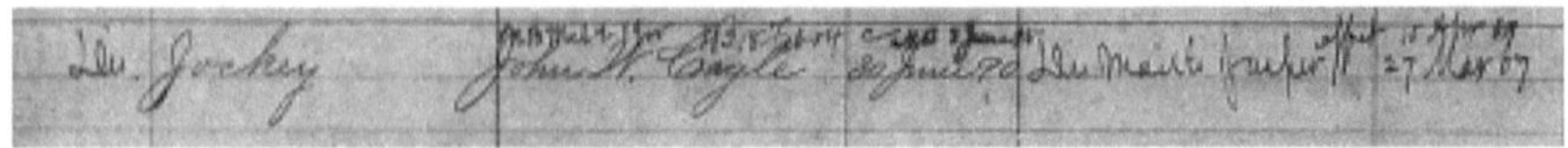

Cagle as seen on the Appointment of Postmasters for Pickens County

According to Alonzo Cagle, the name Jockey was chosen after interaction with men from the area of Jockey, Tennessee who were selling lightning rods. They told him of a post office named Jockey. In the 1880s, their Jockey was a hamlet located in Greene County, Tennesee. *

Like all small post offices throughout rural America, the post office of Jockey was based out of a house. The house, which doubled as a post office and residence, is located immediately southeast of Sharp Mountain Creek, on Land Lot 198 in the Sharp Mountain Militia District.

In February of 1893, during the last weeks of President Benjamin Harrison's tenure, the Postmaster General of the United States, John Wanamaker, mailed a letter of gratitude to John Wesley Cagle for his service.

The 1900 Federal Census lists John Wesley Cagle's occupation as that of miller. According to historian Robert Scott Davis, Jr. John Wesley Cagle helped to build the mill. The Cagle family had bought the land for the site as early as 1869 after a public sale of Mr. Nelson who was murdered by Benjamin McCollum's Raiders. The distillery at the site was one of a handful of Federally authorized distilleries in Pickens County. The Cagle brothers also operated a grist mill, blacksmith shop, furniture store, lumber mill, and Cotton Gin at the site.

The Cagle family used their money from the distillery and other ventures to buy over 1,000 acres of land in what would later become known as Cagletown.

On J.W. Henley's 1903 map of the county, the road just beyond the Jockey P.O. crosses Sharp Mountain Creek headed towards Cagletown.

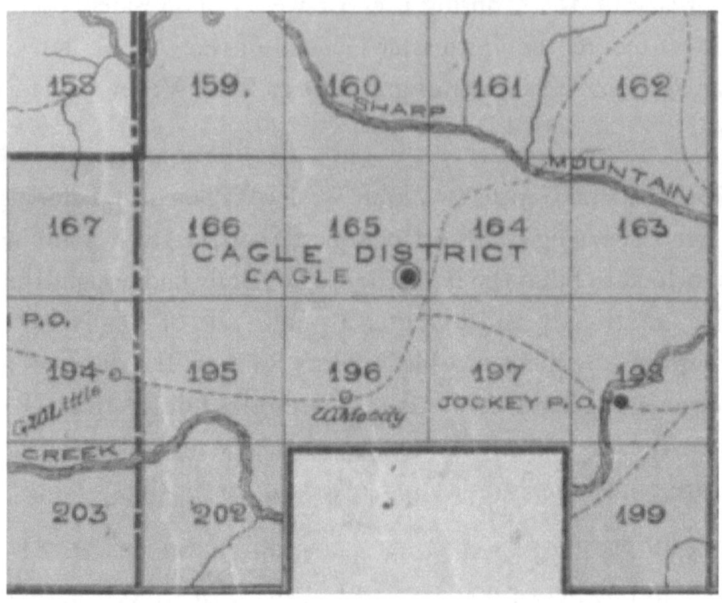

Jockey Post Office as seen on Henley's 1903 map

Eventually, Jockey's post office responsibilities were transferred to Jasper in April 1907.

On the 1926 topographic map of the area, Cagle Mill can be seen on Sharp Mountain Creek. Almost immediately parallel to the Jockey P.O. location.

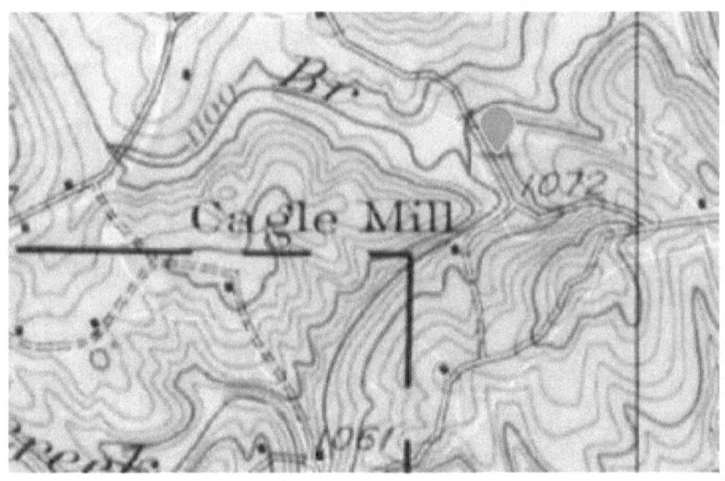

The Jockey Post Office is located at the teal marker

As late as the 1950s the buildings at the Cagle Mill property were still standing. Today, foundation pillars, metal machinery pieces, and ruins of several buildings are visible at the site.

Ruins of Cagle's Mill (2024)

In his later years, John Wesley Cagle enjoyed a more relaxed lifestyle and continued the family tradition of attending Bethany Baptist Church. He attended the church for nearly 70 years. For many of those years, he served as a Deacon and as a Superintendent of Sunday School. According to John's son Tom Cagle, also a Deacon at the church, all the pews were hewn from one tree from his Uncle Peter's property. John Wesley Cagle stayed in the Cagle Mill area until he died in 1949. He is buried at Bethany Baptist Church.

As of January 2024, the house that housed the Jockey Post Office still stands.

*In the *1998 Pickens County Georgia Heritage Book*, it mentions that Alonzo Cagle of Texas, met men working from Tennessee selling lightning rods, and came from a village named Jockey, from which Pickens' Jockey takes its name.

Next to Jockey, in nearby Greeneville, Tennessee, the Lightning Rod King of America, Col. J.H. Doughty resided. He had wagons that traversed most of the southern United States, selling lightning rods in large quantities.

Col. John Harrison Doughty. The Lightning Rod King

As with Col. Sam Tate, Doughty's title was honorary. A successful businessman and real estate purchaser, he had amassed a small fortune, estimated at a half million dollars in 19th-century currency.

Census data shows Daughty family members living in Tennessee, Texas, and Oklahoma. What were their occupations? Lightning Rod Agents. And most likely the same ones that Jockey was named for.

The Tapestry

Looking towards the mountains north

He felt a rush of air burst forth

A bird called him from its nest

Jocular and free, and filled with zest

He was reminded of what had happened here:

Of marble monuments and the trail of tears,

Of the Triple C and the Dude Ranch,

The Whittington home and the Long Swamp Branch.

Of the roads carved by ice and men.

Of the enormity of history beyond his ken.

Of the little things that made him smile,

and the time for gratitude all the while.

The mystery of life all around:

The connectedness of each upon the ground,

the immortality of time beyond our view

and glory of sunsets and morning dew.

Each piece of creation wove its course

into a tapestry of loving force.

The handiwork of God at which he wondered

resounded with peals of mountain thunder.

Afterword

Pickens County offers people a unique opportunity to investigate the past. Unlike the concrete jungles of Atlanta, most of our land (for now) is mostly untouched. As such, there are far more opportunities to find tangible connections to our ancestors. A former mill site, village, chimney, building, perennial garden bed, rock wall, or fence, all leave something behind to touch. Each of those pieces becomes fact, proven by their location, material, and former uses.

Facts are like pieces of filament with each strand intricately linked to another, moving in all directions, but connected to various centers, like a cluster of spider webs in an abandoned house. Each new fact only contains so many subsets of facts. But with enough assembled strands the web fleshes itself out. Each assembled fact pulls us a little closer to the edge of the unknown.

I hope you've enjoyed these vignettes and reassembled puzzles of our past: The good, bad, and ugly all have their place. History cannot be erased by pretending it didn't happen, or by changing the narrative. Once the past transpires, it is etched in stone, immutable and timeless.

To remember the history and travails of our ancestors, we can learn from their hardships and the comforts we take for granted, marvel at the fortitude of our kin, and be grateful for both. And with a little courage and compassion, do our best not to repeat the mistakes of our darkest hours.

Christopher Feldt

Jasper, GA

About the Author

Chris Feldt is a veteran, artist, writer, researcher, poet, composer, and history buff. He moved with his daughter Aviana to North Georgia in 2018.

Read more at https://www.pickenspast.com.